NEW DIRECTIONS FOR CHILD DEVELOPMENT

William Damon, *Brown University*
EDITOR-IN-CHIEF

The Communication of Emotion: Current Research from Diverse Perspectives

Karen Caplovitz Barrett
Colorado State University

EDITOR

Number 77, Fall 1997

JOSSEY-BASS PUBLISHERS
San Francisco

THE COMMUNICATION OF EMOTION: CURRENT RESEARCH FROM DIVERSE
PERSPECTIVES
Karen Caplovitz Barrett (ed.)
New Directions for Child Development, no. 77
William Damon, Editor-in-Chief

Microfilm copies of issues and articles are available in 16mm and 35mm,
as well as microfiche in 105mm, through University Microfilms Inc., 300
North Zeeb Road, Ann Arbor, Michigan 48106-1346.

ISSN 0195-2269   ISBN 0-7879-9895-8

NEW DIRECTIONS FOR CHILD DEVELOPMENT is part of The Jossey-Bass
Education Series and is published quarterly by Jossey-Bass Inc., Publishers,
350 Sansome Street, San Francisco, California 94104-1342. Periodicals
postage paid at San Francisco, California, and at additional mailing
offices. POSTMASTER: Send address changes to New Directions for Child
Development, Jossey-Bass Inc., Publishers, 350 Sansome Street, San Francisco, California 94104-1342.

New Directions for Child Development® is indexed in Biosciences Information Service, Current Index to Journals in Education (ERIC), Psychological Abstracts, and Sociological Abstracts.

SUBSCRIPTIONS cost $65.00 for individuals and $105.00 for institutions,
agencies, and libraries.

EDITORIAL CORRESPONDENCE should be sent to the Editor-in-Chief,
William Damon, Department of Education, Box 1938, Brown University,
Providence, Rhode Island 02912.

Cover photograph by Wernher Krutein/PHOTOVAULT © 1990.

Jossey-Bass Web address: http://www.josseybass.com

Manufactured in the United States of America using Lyons Falls
D'Anthology paper, which is a special blend of non-tree fibers and totally
chlorine-free wood pulp.

CONTENTS

EDITOR'S NOTES

Theoretical views of emotion communication have undergone immense change over the past few decades, in association with changing views of emotion. When emotions were viewed as disruptions that disorganized behavior, they certainly were not viewed as important regulators of interpersonal behavior. When emotions were seen as highly individualistic feeling states with no clear-cut patterns of "expression," they were naturally poor candidates as important vehicles of communication. Then, in the 1970s, when the seminal studies on judgments of facial displays across cultures were conducted (Ekman, 1973; Izard, 1971), a dramatic change took place in the zeitgeist. On the basis of these studies it was widely believed that facial patterns clearly communicate the same emotions to anyone in any culture, as long as rules governing emotional display (display rules) do not interfere with the veridical expression of emotion.

The chapters in this volume reflect some movement away from that positivist stance—a changing zeitgeist. No longer are we content to assume that facial, vocal, or other signals clearly communicate the same emotion in all contexts to all individuals. However, neither do we assume that all facial, vocal, and other signals are random, unrelated to emotion, or uncommunicative to others. The chapters in this volume reflect a diversity of viewpoints—a dynamic systems approach, an emotional security approach, a self- and other-schema approach, and a functionalist approach. Yet all of the chapters in this volume discuss ways in which emotion-relevant responses communicate important information to others.

Four of the chapters (One through Four) focus on emotion communication in the family and how it might affect children's development. Chapter One, by Alan Fogel, K. Laurie Dickson, Hui-chin Hsu, Daniel Messinger, G. Christina Nelson-Goens, and Evangeline Nwokah, outlines a dynamic systems approach to emotion and emotion communication. It is illustrated by research on smiling and laughter from Fogel's lab. Fogel and his colleagues argue that emotion is relational *and not individual,* and that the experience of emotion goes beyond feeling and beyond the limitations imposed by separate corporal entities—that the nonreflexive aspects of emotion do not involve a person and a context but rather the connection between them taken as a whole. The authors emphasize the self-organizing nature of emotion processes, and provide interesting findings regarding social processes involved in smiling and laughter exchanges between mothers and babies in different contexts.

Chapter Two, by Mona El-Sheikh and E. Mark Cummings, pulls together several literatures to demonstrate the similarities between responses of children to interadult conflict and anger on the one hand, and responses of children to living in a family with an alcoholic parent on the other. Noting that children in both environments have problems in regulating emotion, and that children of alcoholics report more conflict and physical violence than low-stress comparison groups, the authors hypothesize that interparental discord may mediate or moderate the effects of parental alcoholism on children's behavior. They propose an emotional security hypothesis to explain these relations, wherein hostile emotion communication may undermine children's sense of security, and as a result, their capacity for emotion regulation.

In Chapter Three, Julie C. Dunsmore and Amy G. Halberstadt present a model for understanding children's formation of self- and other-schemas. In this model, an important role is given to families' tendencies to display emotion or not to display emotion, as well as to their rules regarding the desirability and importance of communicating emotion. Thus, emotion communication in the family is crucial to children's development of concepts of self and other, and in particular, their schemas of how self and other do and should communicate emotion. Children's own characteristics, as well as the cultural context, also play important roles in schema formation, according to this approach.

Chapter Four, by Karen Caplovitz Barrett and G. Christina Nelson-Goens, presents a functionalist perspective on emotion communication and its role in the development of shame and guilt. According to this approach, emotion communication contributes to the development of these emotions through its effects on relationship-building between parent and child; its endowment of significance to standards, rules, and achievement; and its serving as a channel of communication between parent and child regarding standards, rules, and achievement. Research from Barrett's and others' labs is presented in support of the postulates proposed.

The final chapter, by Linda A. Camras, Harriet Oster, Joseph J. Campos, Rosemary Campos, Tatsuo Ujiie, Kazuo Miyake, Wang Lei, and Meng Zhaolan, presents an interesting cross-national study regarding what Japanese, Chinese, and American babies communicate to naive observers in various contexts *when facial information is not available.* Some of the most interesting findings were that cultural differences were manifested primarily in deviations from expected responses to situations: there were cultural differences in *happiness* ratings for the "surprise situation" and in *distress* ratings for the "anger situation." Moreover, Chinese and Japanese babies were not rated as more surprised in the "surprise situation" than in the "fear situation," whereas American babies were. These and other intriguing findings contribute to the growing literature indicating the complexity of cultural similarities and differences in emotional communication.

In conclusion, this volume presents a variety of perspectives and research findings regarding the communication of emotion, broadly defined, during infancy and childhood, and the implications of those findings and perspectives for children's development and for cross-cultural comparison. Emotional communication is an important area of research, and the chapters in this volume provide only a sampling of the new positions and research findings that are available. One implication of all of these chapters, though, is that emotions are communicated in a particular context; the nature of the relationship among communication partners, the cultural background of different communication partners, and ongoing events that are relevant to the communication partners importantly affect what is communicated. Emotion communication within the family and culture has enormous importance for the developing child. We hope that these chapters will inspire more research on these topics.

Karen Caplovitz Barrett
Editor

References

Ekman, P. "Cross-Cultural Studies of Emotion." In P. Ekman (ed.), *Darwin and Facial Expression: A Century of Research in Review.* Orlando, Fla.: Academic Press, 1973.

Izard, C. *The Face of Emotion.* Englewood Cliffs, N.J.: Appleton-Century-Crofts, 1971.

KAREN CAPLOVITZ BARRETT is associate professor in human development and family studies at Colorado State University.

Research and theory related to a dynamic systems perspective on emotion argue that emotions are relational, not individual; self-organizing systems, not generated outputs; and processes of change, not states.

Communication of Smiling and Laughter in Mother-Infant Play: Research on Emotion from a Dynamic Systems Perspective

Alan Fogel, K. Laurie Dickson, Hui-chin Hsu, Daniel Messinger, G. Christina Nelson-Goens, Evangeline Nwokah

In this chapter we present a summary of our recent work examining emotional development in infancy from a dynamic systems perspective. Our goal is to describe the studies that have evolved from our research group and to explain how these studies have been informed by dynamic systems thinking. Reviews of our dynamic systems approach to emotional development can be found in the following works: Dickson, Fogel, and Messinger (forthcoming); Fogel and others (1992); Fogel, Nwokah, and Karns (1991); Fogel and Thelen (1987); and Messinger, Fogel, and Dickson (1997). Additional theoretical discussions of dynamic systems approaches applied to emotion can be found in Camras (1992), Haviland and Kahlbaugh (1993), Lewis (1993, 1995), and Wolff (1987).

We open this chapter with a theoretical overview, followed by a report on our work on the development of emotions related to the expressions of smiling and laughter during the first three years of life in the context of parent-infant play. Smiling is examined in the following social contexts: during face-to-face mother-infant communication (from one to six months), during

This work was supported by grants to Alan Fogel from the National Institute of Health (R01 HD21036), the National Science Foundation (BNS9006756), and the National Institute of Mental Health (R01 MH48680).

normal and experimentally perturbed peekaboo and tickle games (at six and twelve months), and in play activities with mothers and fathers in the home (at twelve months). Finally, we report our studies of the social contextual aspects of the development of laughter in the first three years.

The Dynamic Systems Perspective on Emotion

We begin with a theoretical overview of the major features of a dynamic systems perspective on emotion. The features we emphasize are the following: (1) emotions are relational, not individual; (2) emotions are self-organizing systems, not generated outputs; and (3) emotions are processes of change, not states. We defer giving a concrete definition of emotion until after these features have been introduced.

Emotions Are Relational, Not Individual. How can it happen that emotional experiences are relational even though they are experienced by individuals? Our answer to this question, based on our dynamic systems perspective on emotion, is similar to functionalist theories of emotion in that both theories focus on emotional experiences as relational processes, as arising in the relationship between the individual and the object of emotion (Barrett, 1993; Barrett and Campos, 1987; Campos, Mumme, Kermoian, and Campos, 1994; Frijda, 1986).

When emotional experience is relational, individuals do not perceive themselves as "having" an emotion, because individuals are not necessarily aware of themselves as creating or even as participating in the experience. According to de Rivera (1992, p. 200), "emotions may be conceived as existing between people, as various sorts of attractions and repulsions . . . which transform their bodies and perceptions." According to Frijda (1986, p. 188), emotional experience "is glued, as it were, to its object, coinciding entirely with apprehending that object's nature and significance. . . . [Negative] emotional experience is perception of horrible objects, insupportable people, oppressive events."

This aspect of emotion is called *nonreflective experience,* that is, "awareness without awareness of itself, without some supervisor inspecting it" (Frijda, 1986, p. 188). In Frijda's functionalist theory of emotion, other people and objects are perceived as integral parts of an individual's (nonreflective) experience of emotion. The view of emotion as immediate, nonevaluative, direct experience is also shared by differential emotional theorists (Demos, 1992; Izard, 1991; Tomkins, 1962). "In differential-emotions theory, emotion experience is defined as a quality of consciousness" (Izard, 1993, p. 633).

Emotional experiences are relational but they do not have to occur in the context of live interpersonal relationships. An individual can experience a relationship with inanimate and animate things, with both natural and cultural objects. Relationships can also be remembered and imaginary, and they can be intrapsychic as well as interpersonal and interactive. The important feature for an emotional experience is that there is a meaningful connection that moves the individual, one that establishes the significance or function of the emotional object for the individual in relation to that object (Hinde, 1985; Malatesta-Magai and Izard, 1991).

A contrasting aspect of emotional experience, *reflective experience,* occurs whenever individuals distinguish themselves from others, whenever individuals conceptualize relationships into independent constituents (Frijda, 1986). Reflective experience breaks down the relationship into its component parts and introduces a self and an object into consciousness, changing the experience from direct to analytical (Campos, Mumme, Kermoian, and Campos, 1994).

Emotional experience has both nonreflective and reflective aspects. Reflective appraisals and evaluations can become part of the experience of emotion as individuals evaluate their own history of experience and appraisal (Frijda, 1986). In addition, people can become (nonreflectively) emotional about their evaluations of themselves or others: I can be (nonreflectively) unhappy if I decide (reflectively) that I reacted negatively to another person; I can be (nonreflectively) afraid if I evaluate (reflectively) another's motives as threatening regardless of whether they were so intended.

This alternation between a relational (nonreflective) and an analytic (reflective) mode has been conceptualized by Lewis (1995), for example, as the cycling between cognition and emotion. According to Izard, "emotion experience proper does not include cognition; however, emotion experience is cue-producing, and, as such, it normally recruits the cognitive system" (Izard, 1993, p. 633). From our dynamic systems perspective, there is not a discrete and defined boundary between the relational and analytical aspects of emotion, nor between cognition and emotion. Rather, these two features of experience share a figure-ground relationship that varies with the situation. Sometimes we are more distant, analytic, observational, and controlled, as the figure against the ground of nonreflective experiential flow. Other times we are more caught up in the direct flow of the relationship, which becomes the figure against the ground of our appraisal of the experience.

Because there are many types of relationships, there can be many subtle varieties of emotional experience. Different emotional experiences reflect varieties of relationships with the environment as well as the particular form of action and physiological changes that occur in that relationship. These relational experiences cohere into recognizable emotions and families of emotion (Barrett, 1993; Barrett and Campos, 1987; Campos, Mumme, Kermoian, and Campos, 1994; Fogel and others, 1992; Frijda, 1986).

Emotions Are Self-Organizing Systems, Not Generated Outputs. Emotions are processes that have experiential, sociocultural, and physiological aspects. We use the term *constituent* to refer to any classification of the components of an emotion process. Constituents are conceptualizations; they are abstractions from lived emotional experience. Constituents include the forms of action employed (including the facial expressions, postures, and movements), appraisals and thoughts, ongoing and prior emotions, autonomic processes, central nervous system processes, and relevant features of objects and people (Barrett, 1993; Ekman, 1994; Fogel and others, 1992; Izard, 1991; Izard and Malatesta, 1987). According to Izard (1993, p. 633), for example, "emotion has three levels or aspects—neural, expressive, and experiential—and the term 'emotion' refers to all three components operating as an integral system."

To explain the basis for coherent patterns of relationships between constituents, we use the dynamic systems concept of *self-organization*. Self-organization occurs as constituents act together to constrain the multiple possible actions of other constituents so that the complex system organizes into stable relational patterns called *attractors* (Fogel and Thelen, 1987; Kugler, Kelso, and Turvey, 1982; Prigogine and Stengers, 1984). The relational attractors involve the brain and central nervous system, but there is no reason to assume that the brain is the executive or controller of an emotional process: it is only one constituent of the self-organizing process (Fogel and others, 1992; Messinger and others, 1997; Mischel, Camras, and Sullivan, 1992).

In this view, constituents are not entities with immutable characteristics. Constituents change as they enter into relational processes, altering their independent identities (Barrett, 1993; Fogel and others, 1992). The alteration occurs as changes in the form and function of the constituents. The "memory" of the system is to be found not in learned associations or genetic codes but in the historically preserved changes of system constituents as they become self-organized into a relationship.

For example, the brain changes in both real and developmental time with respect to interactive changes in other people, body movements, and other emotion constituents. Ontogenetically, the brain loses much of its initial openness to input as its function becomes increasingly tailored to the specific experiences of the individual. Rather than thinking of neural programs as the cause or organizer of ontogenetic changes, they can be explained as stable attractors that are the ontogenetic *result* of a self-organizing process (Fogel and others, 1992; Messinger, Fogel, and Dickson, 1997). Phylogenesis provides the raw materials for particular manifestations of emotion, but these materials are processes rather than products, coregulations rather than codes, synergies rather than structures (Prigogine and Stengers, 1984).

In addition, relational attractors that emerge through self-organization are *dynamically* stable. This means that although they are processes that occur in time, they preserve their integrity across a wide variety of conditions. The concept of stability replaces the concept of memory, habit, and association in traditional theories of psychology (see Fogel, 1993, and Thelen and Smith, 1994, for further elaboration). The stability of the system can often be altered under specific kinds of perturbations that force the system to change by making a phase transition from one attractor to another (Kugler, Kelso, and Turvey, 1982; Prigogine and Stengers, 1984; Thelen and Smith, 1994). The relational attractors are encoded neither in the brain nor in the environment. Rather, each time similar conditions recur, the attractor is reconstituted dynamically, that is, by self-organization. This is because the constituents, having changed in order to establish those particular forms of relationship, are predisposed in the future to recreate those same relationships in similar situations.

Finally, we do not have to assume that there is some form of executive control over the formation of attractors in self-organizing systems. The brain, although of crucial importance in any emotional process, is only one constituent in the system. Research in emotional development shows that both behavior and development often appear to be led or regulated by one or another constituent of the system (Fogel and Thelen, 1987; Fogel and others, 1992). While a neural constituent may lead the self-organization of an emotion process at one moment, a motor or social constituent may lead at another time. Dynamic systems perspectives recognize that there are emotion constituents not only in the brain but also in the motor system, the social system, and the physical and cultural environment: all of these are essential to the creation and maintenance of relationships via self-organization (Fogel and Thelen, 1987).

These features of self-organization bear upon the hypothesized existence of a small number of discretely different emotions, as proposed by differential emotions theory (Izard and Malatesta, 1987; Ekman, 1994). As we have argued elsewhere, on the basis of our review of studies of young infants, there are insufficient data on emotional action to conclude that there are a relatively small number of pan-cultural "basic" emotions, regardless of the theoretical position. There are virtually no carefully done behavioral ethologies on which to base inferences about early emotional development in young infants of any culture (Fogel and others, 1992).

If, however, a relatively small number of basic emotions can be shown to exist pan-culturally, we would differ from the differential emotion theory with respect to the explanation for such emotions. In our view, these hypothetical basic emotions would be neither innate nor acquired, nor would they be considered hardwired structures of the brain or body. Differential emotions would be conceptualized as *stable self-organized processes* that tend to recur under particular organismic and functional conditions in a sociocultural environment (Barrett, 1993; Fogel and others, 1992; see also Haviland and Kahlbaugh, 1993; Shweder, 1994; Stein, Trabasso, and Liwag, 1993).

The concept of self-organization has several advantages. First, we can explain why stable and highly regular patterns recur using the concept of dynamic stability of a relational attractor. This requires data on the processes of self-organization in real time rather than a discrete coding of a single facial expression or the labeling of a single emotion removed from its sociocultural and temporal context.

Second, we can also explain the obvious variability in emotion and expression of individuals, groups, and cultures by something more than learned associations. We hypothesize that variability arises because of subtle alterations in the constituents, variations that produce perturbations in the dynamics of self-organization that may predispose the system to make transitions to other attractors or to form entirely new attractors. With time-based data we can potentially explain why some emotions are very stable and others are more labile and variable.

Finally, as shown in the next section, we can explain how change, in real time and developmental time, occurs in emotional processes. Again, research needs to focus on processes of change within relationships (between the individual and a social partner, object, or situation). These relationships can be followed over time, ontogenetically, in order to trace the developmental history of stable emotional attractors, some of which can be interpreted as temperamental or personality configurations (Fogel and others, 1992; Haviland and Goldston, 1992; Lewis, 1995; Magai and Hunziker, 1993).

Emotions Are Processes of Change, Not States. One of the most important contributions of dynamic systems thinking to psychology is that change is conceptualized as an integral part of the everyday action of the system. The psychological system is never thought of as hardwired. In psychological systems, regularities arise from the "soft" assembly of self-organization, and because this is dynamic there is always variability and change (Fogel and Thelen, 1987; Thelen and Smith, 1994).

From this perspective, emotional experience is not only relational; it is also the experience of being a participant in the *creation* of a relationship. Living systems, from cells to organisms, are sustained by creative processes. Creativity occurs whenever attractors emerge via self-organization—attractors that are more than the sum of the constituent parts (Fogel, 1993). Part of the emotional experience is the experience of the relationship coming together (Averill and Thomas-Knowles, 1991; Barrett, 1993; de Rivera, 1992; Fogel, 1993). Creativity does not mean that people can make up emotions anew each time they occur. Rather, creativity refers to the experience of being a participant in a living process that leaves some room for unplanned occurrences and individual flexibility within a system of constraints.

Thus, for example, we experience fear as a change in our relationship to something fearful, with respect to the action readiness for self-protection and the action of escape. Enjoyment is the experience of a change in one's appreciation for and possibly one's movement closer to an object, person, or situation to which the experience is related. Infants, for example, will smile and laugh when they are able to kick freely following the removal of their clothes, an appreciation of a change from one situation to another.

Finally, a major implication of thinking about emotion as the experience of change is that we can better understand the foundations of emotional development. The dynamic systems perspective assumes that when emotional constituents (such as facial expressions) develop, it is attributable to some change or alteration in the self-organizing process by which the constituents coordinate their mutual relationship. *Development* is conceptualized as a change in how a system's constituents influence one another to create a newly emergent set of relational attractors. This is contrasted with the traditional view of development as a change in the set of associations between immutable components or the appearance of new fixed structures. The resulting relational attractors are new self-organizations of the same mutually constraining constituents— although these constituents have changes in relation to one another—rather than the activation of new executive controls (Fogel and Thelen, 1987; Thelen and Smith, 1994).

As a result of repeated experiences of change, we become aware of increasingly subtle aspects of change, including our own development over time. Our emotions develop not only with respect to awareness of relational processes but also with respect to our own role in the creation of those relational processes. Emotions, as they shift between reflective and nonreflective forms of experience, are significant in the perception of our own subjectivity, our self as a creative (or noncreative) participant in a relational process (Fogel, 1993, 1996; Frijda, 1986; Haviland and Kahlbaugh, 1993).

Human Emotion in Everyday Activities

In this section we move beyond a general description of the theoretical principles to discuss how they might apply to human emotional processes in everyday life. According to our theory, the systemic unit of emotional experience is neither the individual nor particular actions or expressions (constituents) but, instead, dynamically stable relational attractors. What are these relational attractors in human emotional processes? We propose that they are *communication frames*.

In social communication, frames are segments of co-action that have a coherent theme, that take place in a specific location, and that involve particular forms of *co-orientation* between participants. Examples of frames are greetings, topics of conversation, conflicts, or children's social games. The meaning of an action in a conflict, for example, is related to features of the conflict frame, including the history of conflicts with a particular partner, the cultural rules for argumentation, and the relation of the particular actions to those just prior and those next likely to occur (Bateson, 1955; Fogel, 1993; Goffman, 1974; Kendon, 1985). In nonsocial communication, frames are the forms of everyday engagement with cultural tools and artifacts, and with the natural environment.

Frames are coherent patterns, attractors, that result from self-organizing processes. Frames are the locus of making actions meaningful, and they provide the stable background of regularity against which novelty (creativity) is perceived to emerge. Because they have a direction of flow across time, frames make action inherently oriented toward something that is about to occur. If we place our prior discussion of emotion into the context of frames, then *emotional experience is the psychological meaning of participation in a relational frame.*

The specific type of emotional process is closely tied to qualitative differences in the communication process within the frame. Positive emotions are more likely to occur when the frame involves mutual participation, when partners are each creatively elaborating the theme of the frame, and when there is a balance in their contributions to the frame. Negative emotion is more likely to occur when frames are coercive, when one partner exerts undue control that leads to withdrawal or resistance of the others (Fogel, Walker, and Dodd, 1997). The quality of emotion also depends on whether frames are part of ongoing relationships, and then on whether they are newly emergent or have a history within the relationship (Fogel and Lyra, forthcoming). In the research reviewed in this chapter we show how different types of positive emotion are related to specific features of the communication process during parent-infant interaction.

The concept of frame is similar to that of *narrative*, used when discussing linguistic communication. Narratives provide the framework by which each of their constituent actions and events share some meaningful relationship; they have a stable theme that emerges from the self-organization of the constituents; and they have an orientational direction of flow over time that motivates the movements of the actors, actions, and events (Hermans and Kempen, 1993; Haviland and Kahlbaugh, 1993; Jones, 1990; Ricoeur, 1983).

A number of emotion scholars have pointed to narrative themes as providing the minimal systemic unit of emotional experience. Tomkins (1962, 1978), for example, suggested that emotions arise dynamically with respect to the direction of changing contours of arousal activation that are embedded within narrative-like scripts and scenes within scripts, where scene and script are taken in the dramatic sense. Demos (1982) has described emotion processes that are embedded in scripts of mother-infant play and has followed stability and change of emotion scripts within dyads. For Stern (1985, 1995), emotions are related to contours of activation with respect to changing dynamics in the creation of narrative-like action structures, called *protonarrative envelopes,* particularly those that occur in communication with others. For Ginsburg (1985), emotions arise with respect to directional sequences along *situated lines of action* in a context. Frijda (1986) suggests that emotions emerge in relationships with respect to the dynamic negotiation of individuals' concerns (thematic orientations of the individual), which direct the individual toward particular types of relationship. Sarbin (1986) argues that emotions have the form of a narrative because people generally describe and interpret their emotional experiences with respect to stories having a dramatic tension, rather than referring to their emotions in terms of simple stimuli and responses.

Emotions, therefore, are integral to the frame in which they occur. A dynamic systems perspective suggests that the whole frame, not any single action or event, should be the focus of research on emotion. In the next section, we review our own research with respect to these theoretical principles.

Summary of Research Findings

Development of Positive Emotion During Face-to-Face Play in the First Six Months. By three months of age, infants are capable of displaying a wide range of emotional expressions during face-to-face play with their mothers. Like other scholars (Barrett and Campos, 1987; Izard and Malatesta, 1987; Sroufe, 1979), we believe that these expressions are related to emotional experience. However, we do not believe that each expression has discrete meaning. From a dynamic systems perspective, different relational and temporal sequences could contribute to different meanings of anatomically identical smiles, and these different sequences could further amplify the differences in meaning between anatomically different smiles.

When and how do anatomically different types of smiles emerge developmentally during the face-to-face play frame between mothers and infants? Because we were interested in the process of developmental change, thirteen mothers and infants were videotaped playing together weekly when these full-term, normally developing infants were between one month and six months of age. Mothers were asked to hold their babies on their laps and play with them as they did at home. The images of mother and baby were captured with three video cameras that were synchronized into a split-screen display. To document interactive process, we separately coded facial actions that constitute different types of smiles, as well as other social actions such as infant gazing at mother and mother smiling. Facial actions were coded using the Facial Action Coding System (FACS) (Ekman and Friesen, 1978) as adapted for infants (Oster and Rosenstein, forthcoming). FACS-certified graduate students coded smiles, or lip corner raises (AU12), and cheek raises (AU6) caused by the contraction of the orbicularis oculi muscle. A third category, the degree of mouth openness (AU26c-AU27), was coded by undergraduate assistants trained by the FACS coders. In the *Duchenne smile,* both the lip corners (AU12) and the cheeks (AU6) are raised (Ekman and Friesen, 1978). In the *play smile,* the lip corners are raised and the mouth is opened into a jaw drop (AU26c-AU27). Finally, *basic smiles* involve neither cheek raising nor mouth opening.

When compared to smiles without orbicularis oculi contraction (non-Duchenne smiles), Duchenne smiles are associated with self-reported pleasure in adults (Ekman, Davidson, and Friesen, 1990; Fox and Davidson, 1988; Messinger, 1994). Fox and Davidson (1988) found that ten-month-old infants tended to Duchenne smile in response to their mothers who were smiling as they entered a room. Our group data also indicate that infants under six months tended to Duchenne smile when mother was smiling. Duchenne smiles were also prolonged when the infant was gazing at mother (Messinger, 1994).

These results suggest that under six months of age, infant Duchenne smiling is related to frames of visual mutuality, of eye contact and/or mutual smiling. Duchenne smiling is a salient constituent of an experience of positive, visually mediated connectedness between the infant and mother. The same interpretation may also be helpful for understanding evidence on Duchenne smiling in adults. Ekman, Davidson, and Friesen (1990) found that adults did more Duchenne smiling than non-Duchenne smiling in response to pleasant stimuli, such as films of animals playing. Adult Duchenne smiling may arise because adults perceive puppies and gorillas (example from Ekman and colleagues' 1990 data) enjoying themselves during play and imagine themselves participating in that perceived enjoyment.

This does not mean that Duchenne smiles are the only true smiles of positive emotion and other smiles are not. Different types of smiles alternate with one another during positive engagement. In the context of the face-to-face frame over time, for example, non-Duchenne smiles change to Duchenne smiles as infants contract orbicularis oculi (raising their cheeks), and Duchenne smiles become non-Duchenne smiles as this muscle is relaxed. In our data, approximately one-half of Duchenne smiles were immediately preceded by non-Duchenne smiles, and approximately one quarter of non-Duchenne smiles were immediately preceded by Duchenne smiles, all within the same face-to-face play frame (Messinger, 1994). In earlier work we found that during face-to-face play frames gazing at mother and infant smiling were temporally linked, and that the infants tended to cycle between this state and gazing away without smiling (Kaye and Fogel, 1980). Thus the temporal patterns of facial actions within a frame suggest a neglected element of what infants and adults experience as they interact. One hypothesis is that the infants' and mothers' experience of this sequential patterning becomes a stable relational attractor. We believe that this sequential pattern involves changing action orientations toward and away from continued mutual engagement—as evidenced in gazing at mother and smiling and then gazing away and not smiling—as well as cycling between Duchenne and non-Duchenne smiles during these periods of smiling. This sequential patterning achieves dynamic stability because, in the context of the relational frame, the invocation of any constituent (that is, gazing at mother or an infant smile) may lead to the dynamic self-organization of the relational pattern. The emotion, for the infant and the mother, is the experience of the occurrence of a particular type of coherent relational process, and also the experience of creatively increasing the chances that the experience will reliably recur.

Developmental change occurs when this stable relational pattern is disrupted and the same set of constituents reorganizes into a different communicative frame accompanied by different emotional experiences. After about four months of age, infants no longer look for long periods at their mother's face accompanied by extended smiling. No amount of maternal gazing, smiling, or postural manipulation of the infant can return the system to the former stable frame. A new stable frame emerges in which attention is directed jointly toward objects. Thus, in order to understand emotion we need to study the participatory process: how individuals orient to each other through mutually coregulated activities, create different forms of relational emotions, and reaffirm (or fail to) their mutual commitment and attachment.

In other research on the first six months and later we have found that multiple types of enjoyment experiences are associated with dialectically patterned relational frames. For example, the next section introduces the open-mouthed play smile, which began during the first six months. Through its emphasis on multiple forms of positive experience and facial expressions, on sequences of interactive patterns, and on the relational stability of generalized patterns of interaction, a dynamic systems perspective has substantially expanded our appreciation of the sophistication of the emotional life of very young infants.

Positive Emotion in Everyday Activities at Twelve Months. Dickson, Walker, and Fogel (forthcoming) explored the communicative process between parents and their infants by examining infant smiles during different types of parent-infant play. The subjects were thirty-six Caucasian families with seventeen female and nineteen male twelve-month-old infants. Each parent-infant dyad was videotaped playing at their home for ten minutes. The videotaped sessions were coded continuously for smile type (basic, play/duplay, and Duchenne smiles) and play frame (object play, physical play, vocal play, and book reading). We found in this study that relatively few play smiles occurred. Rather, most smiles involving a jaw drop also contained a cheek raise. We refer to these as *duplay smiles.*

Log-linear analysis and descriptive narrative analysis revealed that different types of smiles occurred during different types of play frames. Duplay smiles occurred during physical play and object play frames more often than expected by chance, while Duchenne smiles occurred more often during book reading frames. Our results on the occurrence of play/duplay smiling illustrate the dynamic systems approach.

Play/duplay smiles involve both lip corner retraction and mouth opening. Why should these two actions become self-organized, and what is the possible emotional significance of the emergent relational pattern? First, infants may open their mouths into play/duplay smiles in order to increase their air intake during a physically stimulating activity. In one example from a mother-infant physical play frame, the infant's jaw dropped into a duplay smile and a giggle erupted each time the mother shook his body. The infant's jaw dropped simultaneously as the infant was inhaling deeply, which may help explain the occurrence of play/duplay smiles during physical play. Second, there is evidence that tactile stimulation may help create play/duplay smiles. In one father-infant physical play frame, the infant's jaw dropped into a duplay smile as the father's face touched her stomach. She began to laugh as he tickled her stomach with his face in a side-to-side motion. Her jaw closed into a basic smile as the father withdrew his physical stimulation.

Tactile stimulation alone, however, does not cause play/duplay smiles in a linear manner. An example from a mother-infant physical play frame helps illustrate the dynamic nature of the emotion process. The mother and infant leaned toward each other with basic smiles on their faces as the mother lay on the floor. The infant's cheeks raised into a Duchenne smile as the mother made rumbling sounds. Then the infant's jaw dropped into a duplay smile as the mother shook her head against the infant's stomach. The infant's face changed to a neutral expression just as the mother raised her head away from the infant's stomach. The infant then looked at a toy that was beside her. The mother quickly buried her face in the infant's stomach as she had moments before, yet the infant did not smile. The mother attempted again to stimulate the infant's stomach though the infant's attention remained focused on the block that she was now holding.

Thus, although tactile stimulation is one important constituent in play/duplay smiling, it does not cause the smile. The relational pattern that self-organizes depends on the sequential cycling, the dialectic between the constituents involved in the relationship: between different types of smiling, between smiling and gazing, and between different orientations of the body with respect to the partner. Tactile stimulation is related to the play smile at the beginning of the example just presented; however, later during the same session the constituents make a transition into a different self-organized pattern in which tactile stimulation is not related to play smiling. Other components in the system, such as the infant's increased desire to engage with the block, overstimulation from the tactile component, the mother's facial expressions, temporal patterns, and so on, may have played a key role in the transition from one communicative process involving smiling to another that does not involve smiling.

The emotional experience related to play smiling is created through the dialectical activity between the constituents of parent and infant action, facial expression, and physiological processes. The experience of positive emotion during play smiling varies according to the dynamics of these dialectics within the whole play frame. Shaking, tickling, and nuzzling each have unique temporal and physical features that self-organize with the play smile and other activities to create different types of physical play frames, different relational dialectics, and therefore different emotional experiences. Although we cannot come up with specific names for each of these types of emotional experience, we can recognize that they have a dynamic stability that is entirely relational. We have discovered remarkably complex relational dialectics within these play frames that distinguish one emotional experience from another and that reveal variability between dyads in the forms and creativity of their emotional experience (Dickson, Fogel, and Messinger, forthcoming; Fogel, Walker, and Dodd, 1997).

The Dynamics of Positive Emotion During Peekaboo and Tickle Games. Thus far the results reported suggest that emotional experiences need to be interpreted with respect to relational frames. We have found that there is an emotional dynamic within frames, described earlier as dialectical alternations between Duchenne and non-Duchenne smiles or between play/duplay and nonplay/duplay smiles; between smiling and gazing; and between these smiles and gazes and other frame constituents.

To confirm the theoretical proposition that emotional experiences are closely tied to the dynamics of relational frames, we developed a procedure for experimentally altering the dynamics of activity within two particularly common frames in mother-infant relationships: peekaboo and tickle games.

This laboratory study examines the impact of small perturbations to the flow of social games in mother-daughter dyads when infants were six or twelve months. Dyads were randomly assigned to a control or an experimental group.

The participants were 105 Caucasian mother-daughter dyads. The six-month-old control group (n = 26) included twelve infants, while the six-month-old experimental group (n = 27) had sixteen. The twelve-month-old control group (n = 28) had fourteen infants, and the twelve-month-old experimental group (n = 24) had twelve. Regardless of group assignment, mothers were instructed to play a peekaboo and tickle game with their daughters. The game order was counterbalanced across dyads. Control dyads played the games regularly for six trials. Each trial had a dialectical structure, a sequence of cover (setup) followed by uncover (climax) for peekaboo games, and anticipation (setup) followed by tickling (climax) for tickle games. In perturbation dyads, mothers were asked to change the action in the climax portion of the games, thus perturbing the dialectical balance between the setup and climax. Each perturbed game had two normal trials, followed by two perturbed trials, and the last two trials were played normally. In perturbed tickle trials, mothers set up the game, saying "I'm gonna get you" while moving their fingers toward the infant, but then only pretended to tickle their infants. In perturbed peekaboo trials, mothers altered the game by covering their faces; however, they did not uncover their faces when they said "peekaboo."

Ekman and Friesen's (1978) FACS was used by certified coders to identify three components of positive infant facial expressions that were described earlier: AU12, AU6, and AU26/AU27. Then the data were grouped into basic, play, Duchenne, and duplay smiles. Infant gaze was coded for "at mother's face." We present findings for the control and perturbation groups separately, reporting results that obtained statistical significance using repeated-measures ANOVA.

Control Group. In the control group dyads, across all games and trials, there was more basic smiling in setup compared to climax, and more complex smiling in the climax. In addition, all smiles were more likely to be accompanied by gaze at mother in the climax. The basic smile apparently was connected with anticipation and with establishing a communicative link between infants and mothers that allowed the games to proceed. These findings show that positive emotion is not a unitary phenomenon; instead, it varies dynamically with gaze and other actions as a function of the phase of the communicative process within frames.

Peekaboo and tickle games also differed in their contour over trials. Generally, during tickle games there were more smile and smile-gaze co-occurrences in the first two trials, followed by a rapid decline of smiling over trials. However, peekaboo games began with high smile-gaze co-occurrence and, depending on the type of smile, either remained steady or increased over trials. This pattern held for basic, Duchenne, and play smiles coupled and not coupled with gazing at mother. The opposite was true for duplay smiles: they increased over trials for tickle but decreased for peekaboo.

There were marked differences between frames in contours of positive emotion over trials. These real-time dynamics, as predicted from our systems theory, provide a novel window on emotional processes. Once emotion is viewed as a holistic process of change over time, rather than as a discrete-point response to a stimulus, an innovative way to think about altering and enhancing emotions and their development is opened up.

Perturbation Group. In peekaboo and tickle games, different patterns emerged with regard to infants' smiling (AU 12). During peekaboo games, both six-month-olds and twelve-month-olds smiled less during the perturbed trials than during the nonperturbed trials. After perturbed trials, six-month-olds returned to the level of smiling seen in the first normal trials, while twelve-month-olds did not return to the same level of smiling after the perturbation. During tickle games, six-month-olds' smiling dropped in the perturbed trials, while twelve-month-olds' smiling remained relatively stable across trials. Because six-month-olds showed a significant decrease in smiling during the perturbed trials and returned to initial levels of smiling after the perturbed trials, they appear more reactive to the tickle perturbation than twelve-month-olds. Also of interest is that for both games, basic smiles remained relatively unchanged between perturbed and nonperturbed trials. This suggests that basic smiles may have a communication maintenance function during transition periods in the frame.

These results show that even subtle and brief perturbations disturb the overall amount of positive emotion and the contours of positive emotion across trials. The results also reveal that for all groups except twelve-month-olds during tickle games, the infants returned to prior levels of emotion in trials immediately following the perturbed trials. This means that our perturbation was successful at maintaining the dynamics of the frame while at the same time revealing the close linkages between communicative actions and emotional expression.

Further research using different types of perturbations will be important in revealing the relative stability of these frames. Also, the changing self-organization of the various emotion constituents should reveal how emotional experience relates to the dynamics of the frame. Emotional experience can be inferred, as we have suggested, not from a simple reading of a facial expression but from the dialectical patterning of all of the game constituents as they unfold over time.

Laughter as a Social Process

In this section we discuss our findings on laughter. Generally, the results provide conclusions similar to those of our smiling studies: that expressions of emotions are dynamically embedded within relational frames that make them meaningful, and that those frames are composed of dialectical relationships between laughter and other action constituents. The results reported here come primarily from our longitudinal weekly and biweekly observations of thirteen infant-mother dyads playing in a laboratory playroom over the first year of life, and from such observations of eleven of these dyads during the second year. Three additional observations of nine of the dyads were obtained at age three.

Laughter onset is typically dramatic and sudden, and involves vocalizations, actions, and physiological changes (Nwokah and others, 1993). According to our theoretical perspective, the sudden and dramatic transition to laughter by one or more partners is related to the dynamics of self-organization in the constituents of partner and contextual contributions to the relationship. This transition is often predictable but not precisely so, particularly because there are constant developmental changes in the constituents of laughter during the first three years.

According to our data, infants produce their first laugh in the context of infant-caregiver interaction at anywhere from ten to twenty-one weeks of age (Nwokah, Hsu, Dobrowolska, and Fogel, 1994). Early pseudolaughter is highly variable and may show some qualities of quasi-resonant vocalizations (Oller, 1986; Nathani and Stark, 1995) as a result of the limited respiratory and anatomical oral-motor constraints of the infant (Nwokah, Hsu, Dobrowolska, and Fogel, 1994). However, mothers are able to recognize, label, and comment on their infants' first laughs (Nwokah and Fogel, 1993). Once laughter emerges in the infant's vocal repertoire, it becomes a frequent part of the repetitive interactions between mother and infant, with many mothers producing five to twenty laughs and infants one to four laughs in a ten-minute face-to-face play session. During the first two years we found a peak in the frequency of maternal laughter for each mother during the months between the onset of infant laughter at three to four months and six months of age, when infant crawling typically reduces the frequency of face-to-face interactions (Nwokah and Fogel, 1993; Nwokah, Hsu, Dobrowolska, and Fogel, 1994).

Much as we found different types of smiling, we found different forms of infant laughter, such as comment (one peak), chuckle (two peaks), rhythmical (several peaks), and squeal (high fundamental frequency), using acoustic analysis. Also, similar to our findings on the differential occurrence of different smile types within different play frames, we found that different forms of laughter are generally associated with different relational frames. Rhythmical laughs, for example, occur more frequently during mother-infant social play frames, while comment and chuckle laughs occur more frequently in object exploratory frames, both object play alone and joint object play (Nwokah, Hsu, Davies, and Fogel, 1991; Nwokah, Davies, Hsu, and Fogel, 1993).

By one year of age, infant and mother can anticipate that by dialectically alternating their tone of voice, facial expressions, and actions, they can build up to a laugh. Mothers pretend to be angry or stern and chase the toddler, who giggles. The toddler teases the mother by doing something potentially dangerous, like standing on top of the slide but constantly referencing the mother and modulating what she or he is doing while laughing at the mother's concern. Although mothers can encourage a sudden laugh or build-up to laughter in the infant by incongruity such as putting a toy on their own head, such factors as the timing, element of surprise, and attention of the infant are also important. What might change to laughter on one occasion may not do so on another.

The consolidation of the mother-infant socioemotional relationship is also shown by developmental changes in the temporal characteristics of shared laughter. By the second year, the duration of maternal and infant laughter becomes more similar within dyads. In addition, the overlap of co-occurring laughs by the two partners becomes increasingly simultaneous, reflecting an increase in mutually coregulated frames and improvements in the infant's speed of vocal response (Nwokah, Hsu, Dobrowolska, and Fogel, 1994; Stern, 1985).

The dialectics of laughter and gaze also show developmental change. Before age six months, the infant nearly always looks at the mother's face while laughing during game playing. From six to twelve months, infants look at the mother's face before and during shared and infant-only laughter in different social frames. If the activity is a social play frame, the infant looks away after laughing. However, after twelve months the infant is more likely to be looking away or at an object during laughter, both in game playing and during infant actions. Very brief gaze or glancing behavior at the mother by the infant is more likely to occur a few seconds after the child laughs, regardless of age.

Toward the end of the second year, a new developmental milestone is achieved: the onset of first words. The frequency of different facial expressions does not decrease at this time but continues to form the basic emotional foundation for the emergence of verbal communication (Bloom, 1993). Does laughter then exist as another vocal option? As infants develop perceptual and articulatory skills, they begin to combine laughter with the production of words or wordlike utterances (jargon) to create new possibilities for expressing intense affect while speaking (Nwokah and others, 1993). What develops from spoken words and vocal laughter is a combined signal containing some acoustic features of both speech and laughter.

Future studies may better determine how the pragmatic social function of laughter evolves in the context of a variety of daily frames and how individualized laughter styles emerge from the ongoing dynamics of the dyadic relationship. The results so far show that laughter, like smiling, as a constituent of positive emotional experience, varies in both form and dynamics. Laughter, like smiling, is a constituent in a large variety of relational patterns in the context of different frames. Finally, laughter, like smiling, is observed to alternate dialectically with other forms of action. This suggests that the quality of the emotional experience of laughter is not the same over all instances of the expression, and can be interpreted only with reference to the dynamics of the relational frame.

Discussion

In this chapter we have reviewed our research on emotional development in infancy from a dynamic systems perspective. We have proposed that emotional experiences are related to the self-organization of constituents in a relational frame. The relational frame occurs over some finite period, is created with respect to particular forms of action and arousal, and is composed of an alternating dialectic between different types of actions and physiological processes. We have suggested that frames are a reasonable unit of emotional analysis, and that emotion-related actions can be interpreted with respect to the dynamic processes occurring in the frame, taken as a whole.

We discovered that many frames for positive emotion are dynamically stable over real time and developmental time and under the influence of certain types of perturbation. Developmental change can be understood with respect to the dynamics of transitions between frames and the emergence of novel frames in a relationship. In addition, this work also suggests that other frames may exist that are relatively unstable, and their role in emotional experience and its development requires further investigation. Furthermore, stability of frames may not always be adaptive if it is more functional for them to change (Lewis, 1995). Thus the concepts of our dynamic systems perspective have the potential to illuminate both normal and pathological emotional developmental processes.

References

Averill, J. R., and Thomas-Knowles, C. "Emotional Creativity." In K. T. Strongman (ed.), *International Review of Studies on Emotion*, Vol. 1. New York: Wiley, 1991.

Barrett, K. C. "The Development of Nonverbal Communication of Emotion: A Functionalist Perspective." *Journal of Nonverbal Behavior*, 1993, *17*, 145–169.

Barrett, K. C., and Campos, J. J. "Perspectives on Emotional Development II: A Functionalist Approach to Emotions." In J. D. Osofsky (ed.), *Handbook of Infant Development*. (2nd ed.) New York: Wiley, 1987.

Bateson, G. "The Message: 'This Is Play.' " In B. Schaffner (ed.), *Group Processes*, Vol. 2. Madison, N.J.: Madison Printing, 1955.

Bloom, L. "Developments in Expression: Affect and Words in the Single Word Period." In L. Bloom (ed.), *The Transition from Infancy to Language: Acquiring the Power of Expression*. New York: Cambridge University Press, 1993.

Campos, J. J., Mumme, D. L., Kermoian, R., and Campos, R. G. "A Functionalist Perspective on the Nature of Emotion." In N. A. Fox (ed.), *The Development of Emotion Regulation: Biological and Behavioral Considerations*. Monographs of the Society for Research in Child Development, 1994, *59* (2–3, serial no. 240), pp. 2–3.

Camras, L. A. "Expressive Development and Basic Emotions." *Cognition and Emotion*, 1992, *6*, 269–283.

de Rivera, J. "Emotional Climate: Social Structure and Emotional Dynamics." In K. T. Strongman (ed.), *International Review of Studies on Emotion*, Vol. 2. New York: Wiley, 1992.

Demos, E. V. "Facial Expressions of Infants and Toddlers: A Descriptive Analysis." In T. Field and A. Fogel (eds.), *Emotion and Early Interaction*. Hillsdale, N.J.: Erlbaum, 1982.

Demos, E. V. "The Early Organization of the Psyche." In J. W. Barron, M. N. Eagle, and D. L. Wolitzky (eds.), *Interface of Psychoanalysis and Psychology*. Washington, D.C.: American Psychological Association, 1992.

Dickson, K. L., Fogel, A., and Messinger, D. "The Development of Emotion from a Social Process View." In M. F. Mascolo and S. Griffen (eds.), *What Develops in Emotional Development?* New York: Plenum, forthcoming.

Dickson, K. L., Walker, H., and Fogel, A. "The Relationship Between Smile-Type and Play-Type During Parent-Infant Play." *Developmental Psychology*, forthcoming.

Ekman, P. "All Emotions Are Basic." In P. Ekman and R. J. Davidson (eds.), *The Nature of Emotion: Fundamental Questions*. New York: Oxford University Press, 1994.

Ekman, P., Davidson, R. J., and Friesen, W. "The Duchenne Smile: Emotional Expression and Brain Physiology II." *Journal of Personality and Social Psychology*, 1990, *58*, 342–353.

Ekman, P., and Friesen, W. V. *Facial Action Coding System: A Technique for the Measurement of Facial Movement*. Palo Alto, Calif.: Consulting Psychologists Press, 1978.

Fogel, A. *Developing Through Relationships*. Chicago: University of Chicago Press, 1993.

Fogel, A. "Relational Narratives of the Pre-Linguistic Self." In P. Rochat (ed.), *The Self in Early Infancy: Theory and Research*. New York: Elsevier, 1996.

Fogel, A., and Lyra, M. "Dynamics of Development in Relationships." In F. Masterpasqua and P. Perna (eds.), *The Psychological Meaning of Chaos: Self-Organization in Human Development and Psychotherapy*. Washington, D.C.: American Psychological Association, forthcoming.

Fogel, A., Nwokah, E., Dedo, J. Y., Messinger, D., Dickson, K. L., Matusov, E., and Holt, S. A. "Social Process Theory of Emotion: A Dynamic Systems Approach." *Social Development*, 1992, *1*, 123–142.

Fogel, A., Nwokah, E., and Karns, J. "Parent-Infant Games as Dynamic Social Systems." In K. B. MacDonald (ed.), *Parents and Children Playing*. Albany, N.Y.: State University of New York Press, 1991.

Fogel, A., and Thelen, E. "Development of Early Expressive and Communicative Action: Reinterpreting the Evidence from a Dynamic Systems Perspective." *Developmental Psychology*, 1987, *23*, 747–761.

Fogel, A., Walker, H., and Dodd, D. "Beyond Individuals: A Relational-Historical Approach to Theory and Research on Communication." Unpublished manuscript, 1997.

Fox, N., and Davidson, R. J. "Patterns of Brain Electrical Activity During Facial Signs of Emotion in Ten Month Old Infants." *Developmental Psychology*, 1988, *24*, 230–236.

Frijda, N. *The Emotions*. New York: Cambridge University Press, 1986.

Ginsburg, G. P. "The Analysis of Human Action: Current Status and Future Potential." In G. P. Ginsburg, M. L. Brenner, and M. von Cranach (eds.), *Discovery Strategies in the Psychology of Action*. London: Academic Press, 1985.

Goffman, E. *Frame Analysis: An Essay on the Organization of Experience*. Cambridge, Mass.: Harvard University Press, 1974.

Haviland, J. M., and Goldston, R. B. "Emotion and Narrative: The Agony and the Ecstasy." In K. T. Strongman (ed.), *International Review of Studies on Emotion*, Vol. 2. New York: Wiley, 1992.

Haviland, J. M., and Kahlbaugh, P. "Emotion and Identity." In M. Lewis and J. M. Haviland (eds.), *Handbook of Emotions*. New York: Guilford Press, 1993.

Hermans, H.J.M., and Kempen, H.J.G. *The Dialogical Self: Meaning as Movement*. Orlando, Fla.: Academic Press, 1993.

Hinde, R. "Expression and Negotiation." In G. Zivin (ed.), *The Development of Expressive Behavior*. Orlando, Fla.: Academic Press, 1985.

Izard, C. E. *The Psychology of Emotions*. New York: Plenum, 1991.

Izard, C. E. "Organizational and Motivational Functions of Discrete Emotions." In M. Lewis and J. M. Haviland (eds.), *Handbook of Emotions*. New York: Guilford Press, 1993.

Izard, C. E., and Malatesta, C. Z. "Perspectives on Emotional Development I: Differential Emotions Theory of Early Emotional Development." In J. Osofsky (ed.), *Handbook of Infant Development*. (2nd ed.) New York: Wiley, 1987.

Jones, D. *The Matrix of Narrative: Family Systems and the Semiotics of Story*. Hawthorne, N.Y.: Mouton de Gruyter, 1990.

Kaye, K., and Fogel, A. "The Temporal Structure of Face-to-Face Communication Between Mothers and Infants." *Developmental Psychology*, 1980, *16*, 454–464.

Kendon, A. "Behavioral Foundations for the Process of Frame Attunement in Face-to-Face Interaction." In G. P. Ginsburg, M. Brenner, and M. von Cranach (eds.), *Discovery Strategies in the Psychology of Action*. Orlando, Fla.: Academic Press, 1985.

Kugler, P. N., Kelso, J.A.S., and Turvey, M. T. "On Coordination and Control in Naturally Developing Systems." In J.A.S. Kelso and J. E. Clark, (eds.), *The Development of Movement Coordination and Control.* New York: Wiley, 1982.

Lewis, M. D. "Emotion-Cognition Interactions in Early Development." *Cognition and Emotion,* 1993, 7, 145–170.

Lewis, M. D. "Cognition-Emotion Feedback and the Self-Organization of Developmental Paths." *Human Development,* 1995, 38, 71–102.

Magai, C., and Hunziker, J. "Tolstoy and the Riddle of Developmental Transformation: A Life-Span Analysis of the Role of Emotions in Personality Development." In M. Lewis and J. M. Haviland (eds.), *Handbook of Emotions.* New York: Guilford Press, 1993.

Malatesta-Magai, C., and Izard, C. "View I: The Perspective from Differential Emotions Theory." In K. T. Strongman (ed.), *International Review of Studies on Emotion,* Vol. 1. New York: Wiley, 1991.

Messinger, D. S. "The Development of Smiling: A Dynamic Systems Approach." Unpublished doctoral dissertation, Department of Psychology, University of Utah, 1994.

Messinger, D., Fogel, A., and Dickson, K. L. "A Dynamic Systems Approach to Infant Facial Action." In J. A. Russell and F. M. Dols (eds.), *The Psychology of Facial Expression.* New York: Cambridge University Press, 1997.

Mischel, G. F., Camras, L. A., and Sullivan, G. "Infant Interest Expressions as Coordinative Structures." *Infant Behavior and Development,* 1992, 15, 347–358.

Nathani, S., and Stark, R. "Infant Vocalizations in Home and Laboratory Settings." Paper presented at American Speech-Language-Hearing Association Annual Convention, Orlando, Fla., Dec. 1995.

Nwokah, E., Davies, P., Hsu, H. and Fogel, A. "The Integration of Speech and Laughter in Vocal Communication." Paper presented at the American-Speech-Language-Hearing Association Annual Convention, Anaheim, Calif., Nov. 1993.

Nwokah, E., Davies, P., Islam, A., Hsu, H, C., and Fogel, A. "Vocal Affect in Three-Year-Olds: A Quantitative Acoustic Analysis of Child Laughter." *Journal of the Acoustical Society of America,* 1993, 94, 3076–3090.

Nwokah, E., and Fogel, A. "Laughter in Mother-Infant Emotional Communication." *Humor: International Journal of Humor Research,* 1993, 6, 137–161.

Nwokah, E., Hsu, H., Davies, P., and Fogel, A. "Stability and Change in Infant Laughter." Paper presented at the biennial meeting of the Society for Research in Child Development, Seattle, Wash., Apr. 1991.

Nwokah, E., Hsu, H., Dobrowolska, O., and Fogel, A. "The Development of Laughter in Mother-Infant in Communication: Timing Parameters and Temporal Sequences." *Infant Behavior and Development,* 1994, 16, 23–25.

Oller, D. K. "Metaphonology and Infant Vocalizations." In B. Lindblom and R. Zetterstrom (eds.), *Precursors of Early Speech.* New York: Stockton Press, 1986.

Oster, H., and Rosenstein, D. *Baby FACS: Analyzing Facial Movement in Infants.* Palo Alto, Calif.: Consulting Psychologists Press, forthcoming.

Prigogine, I., and Stengers, I. *Order Out of Chaos: Man's New Dialogue with Nature.* New York: Bantam Books, 1984.

Ricoeur, P. *Time and Narrative,* Vol. 1 (K. McLaughlin and D. Pellauer, trans.). Chicago: University of Chicago Press, 1983.

Sarbin, T. R. *Narrative Psychology: The Storied Nature of Human Conduct.* New York: Praeger, 1986.

Shweder, R. A. "You're Not Sick, You're Just in Love": Emotion as an Interpretive System." In P. Ekman and R. J. Davidson (eds.), *The Nature of Emotion.* New York: Oxford University Press, 1994.

Sroufe, A. "Socioemotional Development." In J. Osofsky (ed.), *Handbook of Infant Development.* New York: Wiley, 1979.

Stein, N. L., Trabasso, T., and Liwag, M. "The Representation and Organization of Emotional Experience: Unfolding the Emotion Episode." In M. Lewis and J. M. Haviland (eds.), *Handbook of Emotions.* New York: Guilford Press, 1993.

Stern, D. *The Interpersonal World of the Infant.* New York: Basic Books, 1985.

Stern, D. *The Motherhood Constellation.* New York: Basic Books, 1995.

Thelen, E., and Smith, L. *A Dynamic Systems Approach to the Development of Cognition and Action.* Cambridge, Mass.: Massachusetts Institute of Technology Press, 1994.

Tomkins, S. *Affect, Imagery and Consciousness,* Vol. 1. New York: Springer, 1962.

Tomkins, S. S. "Script Theory: Differential Magnification of Affects." In H. E. Howe, Jr., and R. A. Dunstbier (eds.), *Nebraska Symposium on Motivation.* Lincoln: University of Nebraska Press, 1978.

Wolff, P. H. *Behavioral States and the Expressions of Emotion in Early Infancy.* Chicago: University of Chicago Press, 1987.

ALAN FOGEL *is professor in the Department of Psychology at the University of Utah.*

K. LAURIE DICKSON *is assistant professor in the Department of Psychology at Northern Arizona University.*

HUI-CHIN HSU *is a research associate in the Department of Psychology at the University of Utah.*

DANIEL MESSINGER *is assistant professor in the Departments of Pediatrics and Psychology at the University of Miami.*

G. CHRISTINA NELSON-GOENS *is a doctoral candidate in the psychology department at the University of Utah.*

EVANGELINE NWOKAH *is program director at the Richardson Development Center in Dallas, Texas.*

The role of marital conflict as a mediator of parental drinking problems and of children's emotional regulation and adjustment is highlighted.

Marital Conflict, Emotional Regulation, and the Adjustment of Children of Alcoholics

Mona El-Sheikh, E. Mark Cummings

Understanding the effects of parental alcoholism on children is of interest to both practitioners and researchers concerned with family functioning. Relations between parental alcoholism and a wide range of childhood problems have been documented (see, for example, Roosa and others, 1988; Sher, Walitzer, Wood, and Brent, 1991; Wallace, 1987; West and Prinz, 1987). Indicating the scope of the problem, studies report that between seven million and twenty-eight million children of alcoholics (COAs) reside in the United States (Wallace, 1987), and between 16 and 24 percent of children of elementary school age are from alcoholic families (Woodside, 1988).

Until recently the COA literature was dominated by clinical observations (Black, 1979; Wilson and Orford, 1978) and popular views regarding the traumatizing effects of being reared in an alcoholic family. A main effects model regarding the impact of alcoholism on children was implicit in these treatments (Tubman, 1993), with parental recovery and other environmental variables often not considered as either ameliorating or exacerbating the negative effects of parental drinking.

The extent of adjustment problems varies, however, with many COAs not experiencing psychopathology (Bennett, Wolin, and Reiss, 1988; Clair and Genest, 1987; Moos and Billings, 1982; Sher, 1991; West and Prinz, 1987), which suggests the importance of moderating and mediating variables in relations between parental alcoholism and child outcomes (Burk and Sher, 1988;

The preparation of this manuscript was supported by a FIRST award (R29–10591) from the National Institute of Mental Health to Mona El-Sheikh.

Sher, 1991; Tubman, 1993). Accordingly, there is a shift toward more sophisticated theoretical models incorporating various and multiple domains of biopsychosocial functioning, including family characteristics (see, for example, Fitzgerald, Zucker, and Yang, 1995; Sadava, 1995). Such models offer frameworks that can take into account relatively complex relations between parental alcoholism, vulnerability, and resilience in COAs. Further, there are increasing calls for research to isolate and test the mechanisms through which various environmental processes affect COAs (West and Prinz, 1987). From a treatment perspective, if the contextual conditions and mediating variables that elevate the risk for dysfunction among COAs were well delineated, prevention and intervention efforts could be more efficiently and effectively targeted at children and families most at risk for serious dysfunction.

The usefulness of complex models incorporating mediating and/or moderating variables is also supported by recent research (for example, West and Prinz, 1987) indicating that environmental variables significantly influence offspring outcomes (see, for example, Cooper, Peirce, and Tidwell, 1995). Rather than research conceptualizations being limited to pathology/problem models, there is increasing emphasis on the study of "how individuals' behaviors associated with alcoholism affect both the family and the individuals within it" (Beidler, 1989, p. 135). Several variables within family environments that hold promise for explaining the association between parental drinking problems and child outcomes have been identified, including problems of marital emotional communication. In this chapter we focus on the role of marital conflict in the association between parents' drinking problems and their children's emotional functioning. One goal of this chapter is to demonstrate that parental marital conflict is likely to mediate the emotional responding of children of alcoholics.

Another goal of this chapter is to advance theory in this area of work. There has been a remarkable dearth of theory regarding the role of mediating and moderating variables in the relation between familial drinking problems and child outcome, and such theory is increasingly necessary to make sense of the complex interplay of familial variables that have been identified. In this chapter we advance the notion that children's emotional regulation, and in particular their regulation with respect to emotional security, merits consideration as a mediator of adjustment outcomes associated with parental alcoholism. Recently, Davies and Cummings (1994) proposed a theoretical model of children's emotional security in conflictual home environments. It postulates that children's regulation of emotional arousal in the face of marital conflict and other family stressors plays a significant role in their responding to family events (Davies and Cummings, 1994; Cummings and Davies, 1996). The emphasis of this model is on emotionality: its regulation in marital relations (for example, intensity and resolution), how it is managed by the child, and the role of the quality of other emotional relations in the family (for example, parent-child relations) in influencing children's emotional responding to stressors. In this chapter we extend this model to the consideration of the family circumstances and individual development of COAs.

Representative work from two separate literatures will be considered in this chapter: (1) studies specifically targeting parental drinking, marital and family functioning, and child outcomes; and (2) studies of marital conflict and child socioemotional functioning in general, which provide a foundation for further advances in understanding the effects of marital conflict on COAs. Although we acknowledge that genetic factors and various other environmental and familial variables undoubtedly play a role in susceptibility to the development of problems in offspring of alcoholics, this chapter highlights the impact of adults' angry behavior on children in family environments, a topic that is emerging as a particularly promising new direction for research on COAs and other at-risk populations (such as children of depressed parents; see Cummings and Davies, 1994a, forthcoming). Prior to our discussion of the role of marital conflict in mediating the relation between parental alcoholism and child outcome, the adjustment problems of COAs need to be established.

Sequelae of Growing Up in a Family with Alcoholism

Emotion Regulation and Coping. Many areas of emotion, interpersonal functioning, and coping are negatively affected by parental alcoholism. There is evidence that COAs have greater difficulty than nonCOAs (NCOAs) with identifying emotions (see, for example, Black, Bucky, and Wilder-Padilla, 1986; Plescia-Pikus, Long-Suter, and Wilson, 1988) and expressing emotions appropriately (see, for example, Fukunishi and others, 1992; McDonald and Prachkin, 1990). COAs are more likely than NCOAs to exhibit conduct disorders and aggression (see, for example, Jacob and Leonard, 1986; Fine, Yudin, Holmes, and Heinemann, 1976; West and Prinz, 1987), and difficulties in school (Hyphantis, Koutras, Liakos, and Marselos, 1991; McElligatt, 1986; Sher, Walitzer, Wood, and Brent, 1991; Wierson, Forehand, and McCombs, 1988). Consistently, adult children of alcoholics (ACOAs) tend to exhibit high levels of state anger and, in particular, "anger out," which is the disposition to direct anger toward other people (Potter-Efron and Potter-Efron, 1991). Problems with both controlling or managing anger (Potter-Efron and Potter-Efron, 1991) and the use of aggressive coping strategies toward others have also been found at higher rates in COAs than in NCOAs (Jarmas and Kazak, 1992; Black, Bucky, and Wilder-Padilla, 1986). Heightened anger out and aggression could be regarded as difficulties in affect regulation (Dodge, 1991), and they suggest that COAs may have problems in the control of their emotions.

In comparison to NCOAs, ACOAs are more likely to report greater use of emotion-focused rather than problem-focused coping strategies, and to endorse more avoidance or escape strategies in handling problem situations in their families (Clair and Genest, 1987). Further, endorsing fewer problem-focused coping strategies has been correlated with depression-proneness. Other research indicates that ACOAs may exhibit developmental delay in some coping strategies, tending, for example, to use more palliative and emotive coping than confrontive coping until middle to late young adulthood, when their use of palliative coping behaviors increases (Scavnicky-Mylant, 1990).

Internalizing Behavior Problems. In addition to externalizing problems and coping difficulties, COAs have higher rates of anxiety and depression than NCOAs (see, for example, Rolf and others, 1988; Webb, Post, Robinson, and Moreland, 1992; Williams and Corrigan, 1992). Further, ACOAs tend to exhibit alexithymia at much higher rates than the general population (Fukunishi and others, 1992), and alexithymics have difficulties in describing and expressing their feelings, especially negative emotions (McDonald and Prachkin, 1990). The tendency to experience negative affectivity may also increase risk for the children's own future vulnerability to alcoholism (Tarter, 1988). Internalizing behavior problems could be viewed in the context of emotional dysregulation (see, for example, Garber, Braafladt, and Zeman, 1991; Rubin and Mills, 1991), and they indicate that COAs may have difficulties in adaptive emotion regulation.

Interpersonal Functioning in Family of Procreation. There is evidence that suggests the possible intergenerational transmission of marital and family problems in COAs. That is, in comparison to NCOAs, (1) middle-aged COA females report lower levels of family cohesion and satisfaction in their marriages, higher levels of marital conflict in the presence of their children, and higher levels of parental anger and distress (Domenico and Windle, 1993); and (2) ACOAs report less satisfaction with both their marriages and their relationships with their children (Kerr and Hill, 1992). ACOAs also exhibit a higher need for control in personal relationships than NCOAs (Bradley and Schneider, 1990), which may be related to problems in maintaining satisfying relationships (Black, 1979).

Divorces occur much more frequently in families in which one or both spouses has a drinking problem than in nonalcoholic homes (Kerr and Hill, 1992). Alcoholism disturbs family functioning through sabotaging mother-father, father-child, and mother-child relationships (Hyphantis, Koutras, Liakos, and Marselos, 1991). In an investigation of adult attachment patterns, subjects who scored high on the avoidant and anxious-ambivalent scales of Hazan and Shaver's attachment typology, and thus were considered insecure in their adult attachments, were more likely to have a problem-drinking parent than adults with secure attachments (Brennan, Shaver, and Tobey, 1991). In the same investigation, ACOAs were more likely than NCOAs to be fearful and to exhibit fearful avoidance in their adult attachments. Consistently for women, parental alcoholism was associated with an attachment style with the partner that was characterized by separation protest, angry withdrawal, and inadequate use of the partner for support (El-Guebaly, West, Maticka-Tyndale, and Pool, 1993).

Thus, being reared in a family characterized by parental drinking problems increases the risk for problems in children's interpersonal functioning in relationships, including greater emotional insecurity of relationships with parents, spouses, and other significant others. However, such difficulties are by no means inevitable, and may be moderated by children's experiences with their parents. For example, for COAs, receiving a lot of attention from the primary caretaker in infancy and not experiencing long separations from the parent, which are two variables related to the security of the child's attachment toward the caretaker, are associated with fewer major problems in both childhood and adolescence (Werner, 1986).

The aforementioned findings indicate that COAs are more likely than NCOAs to develop adjustment problems, but other factors may mediate or moderate such effects. Before further developing theoretical propositions regarding mediators of adjustment problems in COAs, however, we first explore parallels between the family circumstances and response patterns of COAs, and the reaction patterns associated with such circumstances in research on other populations, particularly with regard to the impact of marital conflict on children.

Children's Responses to Interadult Anger and Conflict

The marital conflict literature indicates that interadult arguments (anger and conflict between others observed by the child; see Cummings, 1987) are stressful for children (Emery, 1982; Grych and Fincham, 1990). Frequent and intense marital conflict has been consistently associated with externalizing and internalizing behavior problems in children (for reviews see Davies and Cummings, 1994; Grych and Fincham, 1990). Interadult arguments have also been repeatedly found to evoke children's sadness and fear (Cummings, Ballard, El-Sheikh, and Lake, 1991; Grych and Fincham, 1993; Hennessy, Rabideau, Cicchetti, and Cummings, 1994), anger and aggression (Klaczynski and Cummings, 1989), overt behavioral distress (Cummings, 1987; El-Sheikh, 1994; El-Sheikh and Reiter, 1996), and physiological reactivity (Ballard, Cummings, and Larkin, 1993; El-Sheikh, Ballard, and Cummings, 1994; El-Sheikh and Cummings, 1992).

A case study adapted from Cummings, Zahn-Waxler, and Radke-Yarrow (1981, p. 1276) shows the sensitivity of even very young children—in this instance, twenty-month-old Clara—to marital conflict. The mother is the narrator.

I was very upset and I wasn't feeling well. The house was a shambles, where the children had been pulling out toys, and the dishes had not been done, and there were clothes on the floor. I put Clara to bed and ran down to the kitchen to put away some things. Dick was in the kitchen and I yelled at him, "I don't care if this house stays a mess forever, I am not picking up another damn thing." I screamed at the top of my lungs. And in a squeaky voice I heard Clara say "Mommy, shut up" about three times.

A second case study, in this instance adapted from Cummings and Davies (1994b, pp. 49–50), concerns a five-year-old girl's responses to anger directed at the mother by an actress; it illustrates further the impact on children's emotional security of even mild expressions of unresolved conflict involving the parents:

> The actress expressed anger at the mother for her negligence in filling out forms. The child showed distress and sadness while looking down at the floor, and her active play stopped. She was preoccupied with the angry scene. She looked to her mother and smiled but the smile quickly faded. After the actress left, the girl said to her mother, "Doesn't she know that it takes a while to fill out forms?" and moved to stand near her mother. After a few seconds she sat on the side of the mother's chair and put her arm around the mother. She paid special attention to how the mother was filling out forms and made comments: "Is your name on the forms now?" "Are you putting circles on them?" She pointed to specific areas on the forms as she spoke. Finally she said nervously, "Are you done with the forms yet?"

Although unresolved interadult conflicts are generally stressful for children, a history of intense marital conflict increases children's negative responses to interadult disputes. For example, in comparison to children from low-conflict homes, boys from hostile marriages evaluated audiotaped interadult arguments more negatively and were less likely to predict positive outcomes to conflict (O'Brien, Margolin, John, and Krueger, 1991); preschoolers (El-Sheikh, 1994; Cummings, Pellegrini, Notarius, and Cummings, 1989) and preadolescents (Ballard, Cummings, and Larkin, 1993) from maritally distressed and highly conflictual homes displayed more overt behavioral distress in response to interadult arguments; girls from high-conflict homes exhibited higher levels of heart rate reactivity in response to interadult conflict (El-Sheikh, 1994); and children of parents with a history of interparental physical aggression were more likely to report physiological arousal in response to conflict (O'Brien, Margolin, John, and Krueger, 1991). Consistently, children who have been exposed to repeated and intense interadult conflict have been found, through longitudinal investigations, to respond to both naturally occurring interparental conflict in the home and simulated conflict by the mother with heightened overt-behavioral distress (Cummings, Zahn-Waxler, and Radke-Yarrow, 1981, 1984).

These results are consistent with the *sensitization hypothesis,* which proposes that repeated exposure to frequent or intense arguments between others sensitizes children to subsequent conflicts (Cummings and Davies, 1994b), leading to increased negative emotional arousal and distress that in turn may be linked to adjustment problems (Davies and Cummings, 1994). It has been proposed that the patterns of arousal and distress associated with responding to repeated conflict "may become a salient segment of the child's behavior and generalize to the child's general repertoire for reacting to stress" (Cummings and Davies, 1994b, p. 57). The sensitization model has been directly tested and supported in relation to children's responding to interadult arguments as a function of prior exposure to interadult aggression (Cummings, Pellegrini, Notarius, and Cummings, 1989), abuse by the parent toward the child (Cummings, Hennessy, Rabideau, and Cicchetti, 1994; Hennessy, Rabideau, Cicchetti, and Cummings, 1994), and adult-child (for example, parent-sibling) disputes (El-Sheikh, 1997). Given that a history of marital conflict has an impact on responding to subsequent interadult arguments (Cummings, Pellegrini, Notarius, and Cummings, 1989), even between strangers (El-Sheikh, 1994), the examination of the effects of exposure to frequent or intense interparental arguments in mediating COAs' emotional responding to stressors in general, and to conflict in particular, is a promising new direction for elucidating the mechanisms of effect between parental drinking problems and children's emotional functioning.

Similarities Between COAs and Children from High-Conflict Homes

Emotion Regulation and Coping. A comparison of the COA and marital conflict literatures demonstrates that many of the problems observed in COAs are also found in children exposed to high levels of marital conflict (see, for example, Emery, Weintraub, and Neale, 1982; Gottman and Katz, 1989; Shaw and Emery, 1987). In comparison to control subjects, children from homes characterized by frequent and intense marital conflict and those from alcoholic homes are more likely to exhibit conduct disorders and aggression (Emery, 1982; Grych and Fincham, 1990; Jacob and Leonard, 1986; Fine, Yudin, Holmes, and Heinemann, 1976; West and Prinz, 1987), difficulties in school (Hyphantis, Koutras, Liakos, and Marselos, 1991; Long, Slater, Forehand, and Fauber, 1988; McElligatt, 1986; Sher, Walitzer, Wood, and Brent, 1991; Wierson, Forehand, and McCombs, 1988), and heightened feelings of anger in response to interadult conflict (Blakeman, 1996; Cummings, Zahn-Waxler, and Radke-Yarrow, 1981). Further, much as COAs are more likely than NCOAs to intervene in interadult conflict (Ballard and Cummings, 1990), children of parents with a history of interparental physical aggression are more likely than children from low-conflict homes to report a desire for self-interference in conflict (O'Brien, Margolin, John, and Krueger, 1991), as well as actual involvement in interadult disputes (Cummings, Pellegrini, Notarius, and Cummings, 1989).

Internalizing Behavior Problems. Frequent exposure to both interparental conflict and parental drinking problems have been related to emotional problems in children (see, for example, Black, 1981; Cummings and Davies, 1994b; Jenkins and Smith, 1991; Moos and Moos, 1984; Sher,

Walitzer, Wood, and Brent, 1991). In comparison to control subjects, COAs and children from high-conflict homes exhibit higher levels of depression (Emery, 1982; Moos and Moos, 1984; Rubio-Stipec and others, 1991) and anxiety (Grych and Fincham, 1990; Shaw and Emery, 1987; Wilson and Orford, 1978). Further, children from high-conflict homes display more distress in response to interadult disputes (El-Sheikh, 1994; Cummings, Pellegrini, Notarius, and Cummings, 1989). Similarly, in comparison to children from low-conflict homes, COAs report much higher levels of experienced sadness in response to interadult conflict (Blakeman, 1996), which may be linked to the development of depression and indicates problems with affect regulation.

Further examination of marital conflict in alcoholic homes will undoubtedly elucidate more about relations between parental drinking problems and child problems. This understanding is in turn essential for a process-oriented understanding of the bases for adjustment problems in children from angry home environments, including COAs (Cummings and El-Sheikh, 1991; Cummings and Cummings, 1988).

Does Marital Conflict Mediate Parental Drinking Problems and Child Outcome?

The aforementioned review indicates that COAs and children from high-conflict homes exhibit similar internalizing and externalizing behavior problems. In addition, marital interactions in alcoholic homes and in nonalcoholic but maritally distressed homes bear remarkable similarities in level of marital satisfaction, number of areas of desired change, hostility, and negative verbal behavior during interactions with partners (Billings, Kessler, Gomberg, and Weiner, 1979; Jacob and Krahn, 1988). Marital conflict, which is considered the best familial predictor of behavior problems in childhood (Emery, 1982), is also found at increased rates in alcoholic homes (see, for example, Bingham and Bargar, 1985; Filstead, McElfresh, and Anderson, 1981; Giglio and Kaufman, 1990; Lund and Dwyer, 1979; Moos and Moos, 1984; Rubio-Stipec and others, 1991; Senchak, Leonard, Greene, and Carroll, 1995; Tubman, 1993). Alcohol consumption, especially heavy use of alcohol, is correlated with men's physical violence against women (see, for example, Cate and others, 1982; Heyman, O'Leary, and Jouriles, 1995; Leonard and Senchak; 1993; Leonard and others, 1985; Makepeace, 1986), and alcohol intoxication is implicated in 50 to 70 percent of spousal battery cases (see, for example, Leonard and others, 1985; Nisonoff and Bitman, 1979). Recovered alcoholics report fewer family arguments (Moos and Moos, 1984) and a decline in the prevalence of marital violence (O'Farrell and Murphy, 1995) in comparison to families of relapsed alcoholics.

In comparison to NCOAs, COAs are more frequent observers of marital conflict, both when the parents are sober and when they are intoxicated (Black, Bucky, and Wilder-Padilla, 1986). Disharmony in the family is more distressing to children than parental drinking itself (Bingham and Bargar, 1985). For example, 85 percent of COAs stated that parental quarrels were their major cause of distress, while only 6 percent reported that parental drinking was most troublesome (Cork, 1969). Moreover, COAs are less adversely affected if marital conflict does not accompany parental drinking (Seixas and Youcha, 1985) and are more resilient when parental conflict is absent during the first two years of the child's life (Werner, 1986). In an investigation of associations between parental alcoholism, adverse family environments (in which marital discord occurred), and children's internalizing behavior problems, Rubio-Stipec and colleagues (1991, p. 85) concluded that "it is difficult to separate the effects of parental alcoholism on childhood psychopathology from that of an adverse environment." Similarly, family stress and dysfunction have been implicated in relations between parental alcoholism and the responses of ACOAs on measures of depression and anxiety (Dodd and Roberts, 1994; Havey and Dodd, 1992). Further, a recent study of ACOAs demonstrated a negative correlation between parental marital conflict and interpersonal skills (Senchak, Leonard, Greene, and Carroll, 1995).

Thus, conflictual home environments may mediate many effects of parental alcohol problems on children (see also Senchak, Leonard, Greene, and Carroll, 1995; West and Prinz, 1987). Further, marital conflict increases the likelihood of other familial risk factors. For example, there is a high co-occurrence of spousal violence and parent-child aggression (Hughes, 1988; Jouriles, Barling, and O'Leary, 1987; Jouriles and Norwood, 1995; McCloskey, Figueredo, and Koss, 1995; Straus and Smith, 1990; Wolfe, 1985). And the occurrence of child abuse has been found to increase the risk for adjustment problems in COAs (see, for example, Giglio and Kaufman, 1990; West and Prinz, 1987; Wilson and Orford, 1978).

However, the study of marital conflict as a mediator of parental alcohol problems is relatively new. The literature is small, and its scientific rigor is often low. In particular, because most of the research has been correlational, the obtained relations between child problems and alcoholism could be attributable to third variables and associated family processes (Sher, 1991). Thus these studies have implicated, but not yet firmly established from a scientific perspective, marital conflict as a primary mediating variable in the association between parental alcoholism and child problems (see, for example, Buwick, Martin, and Martin, 1988; Callan and Jackson, 1986; Cork, 1969; El-Guebaly and Offord, 1977; Tharinger and Koranek, 1988).

The Emotional Security Model

The expectation that exposure to marital conflict may be a significant mediating variable in the relation between drinking problems and child outcomes is supported by the aforementioned literature and is consistent with the emotional security hypothesis. Emotional security refers to some specific contexts of emotional regulation within the more general domain of emotional regulation processes (see, for example, Cicchetti and Izard, 1995; Fox, 1994;

Thompson, 1994). These contexts (discussed later in more detail) are certain conditions surrounding specific emotional relationships in the family, such as the security of the child's attachment to the caregiver and exposure to family violence. The emotional security hypothesis (discussed in more detail in Cummings and Davies, 1996) describes a class or set of children's response processes that have the function or goal of regulating emotional arousal in relation to the children's emotional functioning in the family, and that contribute to the relations between marital conflict and child adjustment. Thus an emotional security hypothesis is a specific theoretical application that specifies certain contexts of emotion regulation.

The emotional security hypothesis postulates that multiple relations within the family have an impact on children's emotional security, which regulates and is regulated by interpersonal behaviors within the family. These relations include the quality of parent-child attachments, and family hostilities such as child abuse and interparental violence (Cummings and Davies, 1996). Intense and destructive marital conflict promotes arousal and greater levels of emotional dysregulation in coping not only with marital conflict but also with other stressors (Cummings and Davies, 1996; Davies and Cummings, 1994). In fact, children have sound bases for emotional insecurity in contexts of high family conflict, discord, and insecure parent-child attachment relationships. In particular, marital conflict can cause family life to be emotionally unpleasant, it can threaten the children's emotional and even physical well-being, it can result in a breakdown of discipline practices, it can reduce the emotional availability and sensitivity of parents to children, and it can have negative implications for the future intactness of the family (Cummings and Davies, 1994b). Thus children's histories of exposure to conflict in the home play a role in the regulation of emotional arousal and in responding in the face of interpersonal stressors (Davies and Cummings, 1994; Cummings and Davies, 1996). Over time the impact of these response processes in the context of parental, intrafamilial, and personal relations accumulates and comes to have significant implications for children's short- and long-term adjustment.

Similar to current functionalist perspectives on human emotion (Campos, Campos, and Barrett, 1989; Campos, Mumme, Kermoian, and Campos, 1994; Thompson, 1994; Thompson and Caulkins, 1996), emotion is seen as functional and central to the regulation of behavior. Felt-security is postulated from the child's perspective and defined from a functionalist perspective, reflecting the entire repertoire and pattern of children's reactions to events in relation to emotional security (overt behaviors, thoughts, reported affect, and physiological responses), as opposed to simply those reactions that are "conscious" and reported as "feelings." Emotional security is a response to the immediate person-environment context, but also to the historical context of the child's experience with familial situations (for example, past exposure to hostility) and the child's biological and temperamental dispositions. Accordingly, a child's problems in emotion regulation in stressful contexts may indicate biologically based dispositions in relation to the intensity of experienced emotions, problems in regulation because of the child's history of exposure to stressors, or the interplay between the biological and experiential variables that undermine the regulation of affect (Cummings and Davies, 1996).

Finally, consistent with a commitment to testable theory, component regulatory processes are specified. Although emotional security is a construct that describes the function of obtaining and maintaining security, it contains various specific processes or components, including processes of emotional regulation once the child is exposed to family stress, regulation of exposure to family affect, and effects of repeated histories of exposure to particular family events (Cummings and Davies, 1996; Davies and Cummings, 1994). These specific processes are separate but also interdependent in their relation to emotion regulation and its impact on emotional security. Children's regulatory processes in relation to the function or goal of emotional security can be characterized in relation to these more specific aspects of affect regulation, which are briefly discussed next (for more detail, see Cummings and Davies, 1996).

Affect Regulation. Affect regulation refers to children's emotional arousal and their capacity to maintain, reduce, or enhance their feelings. Regulation of affect can be inferred from several response domains, including children's subjective feelings, overt expression of emotion, and physiological arousal. Regulation may be inferred from many aspects of children's emotional responding, including intensity of negative affect, latency between the stressor and negative response, and persistence or difficulties in reducing the negative affect after the termination of the stressor (Cummings and Davies, 1996; Thompson, 1994). Further, the pattern of responding, rather than specific discrete responses, is most informative for an understanding of emotional regulation and dysregulation.

Insecure attachment, marital conflict, and physical child abuse, among other family stressors, are each seen as evoking multiple emotional responses in the face of stress, reducing children's capacity to regulate emotionality. For example, children who are either abused or exposed to interparental violence tend to exhibit more intense and more numerous affective expressions when they are exposed to interadult conflict, indicating that they may have emotion regulation difficulties (see, for example, Cummings, Zahn-Waxler, and Radke-Yarrow, 1981; Hennessy, Rabideau, Cicchetti, and Cummings, 1994). Repeated exposure to family stresses lowers thresholds for dysregulation, in part by having an impact on physiological systems associated with regulation (Cicchetti and Tucker, 1994; Post, Weiss, and Leverich, 1994), leading to heightened emotional and behavioral reactivity, that is, sensitization to stressful events. The occurrence of these and other stressful events in families with parental drinking problems would be expected to lead to children's reduced capacity to regulate emotions, particularly in stressful situations.

Regulation of Exposure to Family Affect. Relatedly, another way for children to regulate their emotional security is by their exposure to family affect. Thus, in comparison to children from low-conflict families, those from hostile family environments would be expected, according to the emotional security hypothesis, to be more likely to attempt to regulate their exposure to interparental emotional interactions. This regulation of exposure may be exhibited through chronic avoidance of and escape from family conflict, or through high levels of enmeshment in disputes. Although these strategies of controlling exposure to family conflict may be functional and adaptive in the short term, both chronic enmeshment and avoidance of interparental hostility are associated with child behavior problems (Cummings and Davies, 1994b).

Exposure to Family Interactions in an Alcoholic Home. Finally, children's histories of exposure to family relations based on the relatively stressful family circumstances surrounding parental alcoholism would be expected to play a role in their adjustment to stress. Particularly, such experiences would be expected to heighten children's primary assessment of the negativity, threat, and self-relevance of events, and their secondary appraisal of why each event is occurring, who is responsible, and whether they have adequate coping skills (Grych and Fincham, 1990). Unfortunately, the emotion regulation difficulties and response patterns that children may exhibit in a home environment characterized by parental alcoholism and hostility may persist despite positive changes in the social context. Children's past experiences with conflict and appraisals of family events are thus seen as both reflecting and affecting their emotional security.

In summary, there are bases for expecting children's emotional insecurity to be increased by the marital conflict and other stressful circumstances surrounding parental alcoholism. Each of the dimensions of emotional security provides a means for assessing the impact on children's emotional regulatory processes, with implications for children's risk for adjustment problems.

COAs' Emotional Responding to Interadult Conflict: Evidence Relevant to an Emotional Security Hypothesis

Theoretically, the evidence on the emotional functioning of COAs and their families is consistent, in outline, with the hypothesis that problems of emotional regulation and, in particular, emotional insecurity, mediate the risk for adjustment problems for COAs and their families. As we have seen, marital conflict is heightened in families with an alcoholic parent, and there is greater incidence of insecure attachment relationships. Consistently, emotional security is hypothesized to be a product of past experiences with marital conflict and the security versus insecurity of parent-child attachment (Cummings and Davies, 1996; Cummings and El-Sheikh, 1991; Davies and Cummings, 1994). Furthermore, as previously discussed, COAs have greater problems with regulating their emotional arousal and with responding effectively and appropriately to stressful family situations. We have hypothesized that children's concerns about emotional security, which are a function of their history of exposure to stressors in the home environment, play a significant role in their regulation of emotional arousal and responding in the face of family events; thus these data make sense in terms of an emotional security hypothesis.

Two studies of verbal-emotional responses to simulated interadult angry interactions in six- to ten-year-old COAs (Ballard and Cummings, 1990) and one of adult male COAs (Britt, Tucker, and El-Sheikh, 1995) found some aspects of emotional responding to be influenced by a family history of drinking problems. In Ballard and Cummings (1990), COAs indicated more personal involvement in the resolution of adults' angry interactions, which is consistent with notions in the popular COA literature that COAs take too much responsibility for others' problems and often intervene in disputes either to mediate the arguments or to triangulate and form alliances with one parent against the other (Hanson and Liber, 1989; Wilson and Orford, 1978). Intervening in interadult conflict is typically not desirable for the child in that it is associated with experiencing self-blame (Grych and Fincham, 1993), and self-blame is positively correlated with internalizing behavior problems in girls (Cummings, Davies, and Simpson, 1994). Intervention in interparental disputes is also potentially dangerous for the child because of the high correlation between interadult aggression and adult-child violence (see, for example, Hughes, 1988; Jouriles, Barling, and O'Leary, 1987; Wolfe, 1985). Also, opposite to the pattern typically observed with NCOAs, female COAs reported more anger in response to interadult conflict than did male COAs (Ballard and Cummings, 1990). Note, however, that marital conflict and aggressive tactics, as measured by parental questionnaire reports, were much more prevalent in alcoholic than in nonalcoholic families, and these variables could have mediated children's emotional responding.

In a comparison among adult male NCOAs, ACOAs with a recovered parent, and ACOAs with an actively alcoholic parent (Britt, Tucker, and El-Sheikh, 1995), ACOAs with an actively alcoholic parent perceived relatively more positive emotional expression when the videotaped actors were said to have been drinking during a friendly exchange. Moreover, regardless of parental drinking status, subjects perceived physically aggressive individuals depicted on videotapes as having consumed more alcohol than those who exhibited verbal anger. Further, in comparisons of similar interactions that varied in terms of whether the actors were said to have been drinking, both COA and NCOA subjects perceived lower levels of negative affect, including anger, when they were told that the arguing individuals had been drinking. When considered in conjunction with findings from the alcohol and aggression literature (for example, Cate and others, 1982; Heyman, O'Leary, and Jouriles, 1995; Leonard and others, 1985), this study suggests that individuals who drink heavily may view their drinking as excusing their anger expression, whereas others belittle their intoxicated expressions of anger (Britt, Tucker, and El-Sheikh, 1995). These miscommunications can contribute to the hostile angry interactions often associated with alcohol consumption (Britt, Tucker, and El-Sheikh, 1995).

These results thus suggest that several of the dimensions of regulatory functioning subsumed within the construct of emotional security are affected by parental alcoholism. However, the evidence thus far with regard to these propositions is relatively scant. At a minimum, the research to date highlights the need for further investigations of multiple dimensions of emotional responding among COAs, including physiological, overt-behavioral, and verbal expression, in varying background anger contexts. Very few studies using children as subjects have systematically examined relations between parental drinking problems and children's interpersonal and emotional functioning. These studies tended not to use behavioral observations in assessing interpersonal functioning, and their findings are inconsistent (Sher, 1991). Further, although it is suspected that COAs may demonstrate subtle deficits in interpersonal skills, which "may be acquired during negative family interactions or observations of family conflict," very few studies have examined the effects of parental drinking problems on COAs' functioning through actual participant behavior and objective ratings by external observers, despite the prevalence of behavioral methods in the general interpersonal skills literature (Senchak, Leonard, Greene, and Carroll, 1995, p. 153). In contrast, a few studies that focused on interactions of parents from families where at least one partner exhibited drinking problems have demonstrated the utility of behavioral measures in studying dynamic interactions in family contexts that involve adult alcohol consumption (see, for example, Jacob and Krahn, 1988; Lang, Johnston, Pelham, and Gelernter, 1989).

Studies of physiological reactivity have generally found that, in comparison to NCOAs, adult COAs do not differ in basal levels of autonomic arousal (Finn and Pihl, 1987; Finn, Zeitouni, and Pihl, 1990), but may differ in reactivity to nonaversive stimulation (Walitzer and Sher, 1990) and laboratory stressors (Levenson, Oyama, and Meek, 1987; Pihl, Peterson, and Finn, 1990). Importantly, however, physiological reactivity has not been investigated in young COAs, and most research has focused on a narrow set of response domains. According to Sher (1991), this precludes "our ability to statistically integrate findings across biological, psychosocial, and social domains. . . . Without such an understanding, our attempt to predict who will suffer the adverse effects of parental alcoholism (and under what conditions) will be limited" (p. 171). The emotional security hypothesis provides a framework for future investigations of these issues, and a model for integrating and interpreting responses based on multiple dimensions of responding.

Conclusions and Implications for Future Directions

This review thus indicates increasing bases for the view that family emotional processes associated with alcoholism, particularly marital conflict, are linked with children's adjustment problems. In addition to heightened marital conflict in these homes, and problems of COAs in coping with these events, the response patterns of COAs bear notable similarities to response processes associated with repeated exposure to unresolved parental conflicts in other populations. An emotional security hypothesis is outlined as a theoretical model relevant to parental alcoholism and family functioning that emphasizes the role of emotionality in these family environments. The proposition that children's emotional security is endangered in these relatively threatening social contexts makes sense of various aspects of these data (for example, COAs' greater disposition to intervene) and provides a testable model that can guide much of the future research that is needed on these questions. The research findings and these theoretical propositions about family emotions and emotionality affecting children with alcoholic parents have implications for both how practitioners conceptualize these family environments and how researchers might plan future studies of parental alcoholism, family functioning, and children's adjustment.

References

Ballard, M., and Cummings, E. M. "Response to Adults' Angry Behavior in Children of Alcoholic and Nonalcoholic Parents." *Journal of Genetic Psychology,* 1990, *151,* 195–209.

Ballard, M. E., Cummings, E. M., and Larkin, K. "Emotional and Cardiovascular Responses to Adults' Angry Behavior and to Challenging Tasks in Children of Hypertensive and Normotensive Parents." *Child Development,* 1993, *64,* 500–515.

Beidler, R. J. "Adult Children of Alcoholics: Is It Really a Separate Field for Study?" *Drugs and Society,* 1989, *3,* 133–141.

Bennett, L. A., Wolin, S. J., and Reiss, D. "Deliberate Family Process: Strategy for Protecting Children of Alcoholics." *British Journal of Addiction,* 1988, *83,* 821–829.

Billings, A. G., Kessler, M., Gomberg, C. A., and Weiner, S. "Marital Conflict Resolution of Alcoholic and Nonalcoholic Couples During Drinking and Nondrinking Sessions." *Journal of Studies on Alcohol,* 1979, *40,* 183–195.

Bingham, A., and Bargar, J. "Children of Alcoholic Families: A Group Treatment Approach for Latency Age Children." *Journal of Psychosocial Nursing and Mental Health Services,* 1985, *23,* 13–15.

Black, C. "Children of Alcoholics." *Alcohol Health and Research World,* 1979, *4,* 23–27.

Black, C. "Innocent Bystanders at Risk: The Children of Alcoholics." *Alcoholism,* 1981, *5,* 22–26.

Black, C., Bucky, S. F., and Wilder-Padilla, S. "The Interpersonal and Emotional Consequences of Being an Adult Child of an Alcoholic." *International Journal of the Addictions,* 1986, *21,* 213–231.

Blakeman, B. *Children's Behavioral and Physiological Responding to Angry Interactions: The Role of Parental Alcoholism and Marital Conflict.* Unpublished master's thesis, Auburn University, Auburn, Ala., 1996.

Bradley, L. G., and Schneider, H. G. "Interpersonal Trust, Self-Disclosure, and Control in Adult Children of Alcoholics." *Psychological Reports,* 1990, *67,* 731–737.

Brennan, K. A., Shaver, P. R., and Tobey, A. E. "Attachment Styles, Gender and Parental Problem Drinking." *Journal of Social and Personal Relationships,* 1991, *8,* 451–466.

Britt, R., Tucker, J. A., and El-Sheikh, M. "Social Perceptual Processes in Adult Children of Alcoholics." Paper presented at the American Psychological Association Annual Convention, New York City, Aug. 1995.

Burk, J. P., and Sher, K. J. "The 'Forgotten Children' Revisited: Neglected Areas of COA Research." *Clinical Psychology Review,* 1988, *8,* 285–302.

Buwick, A., Martin, D., and Martin, M. "Helping Children Deal with Alcoholism in Their Families." *Elementary School Guidance and Counseling,* 1988, *23,* 112–117.

Callan, V. J., and Jackson, D. "Children of Alcoholic Fathers and Recovered Alcoholic Fathers: Personal and Family Functioning." *Journal Studies on Alcohol,* 1986, *47,* 180–182.

Campos, J. J., Mumme, D. L., Kermoian, R., and Campos, R. G. "Commentary: A Functionalist Perspective on the Nature of Emotion." In N. A. Fox (ed.), *The Development of Emotion Regulation: Biological and Behavioral Considerations.* Monographs of the Society for Research in Child Development, 1994, *59,* (2–3, serial no. 240), 284–303.

Campos, J. J., Campos, R. G., and Barrett, K. C. "Emergent Themes in the Study of Emotional Development and Emotion Regulation." *Developmental Psychology,* 1989, *25,* 394–402.

Cate, C. A., Henton, J. M., Koval, J., Christopher, F. S., and Lloyd, S. "Premarital Abuse: A Social Psychological Perspective." *Journal of Family Issues,* 1982, *3,* 79–90.

Cicchetti, D., and Izard, C. E. (eds.). "Special Issue: Emotions in Developmental Psychopathology." *Development and Psychopathology,* 1995, *7,* 1–226.

Cicchetti, D., and Tucker, D. "Development and Self-Regulatory Structures of the Mind." [Special Issue: Neural Plasticity, Sensitive Periods, and Psychopathology.] *Development and Psychopathology,* 1994, *6,* 533–549.

Clair, D., and Genest, M. "Variables Associated with the Adjustment of Offspring of Alcoholic Fathers." *Journal of Studies on Alcohol,* 1987, *48,* 345–355.

Cooper, M. L., Peirce, R. S., and Tidwell, M-C.O. "Parental Drinking Problems and Adolescent Offspring Substance Use: Moderating Effects of Demographic and Familial Factors." *Psychology of Addictive Behaviors,* 1995, *9,* 36–52.

Cork, R. M. *The Forgotten Children.* Toronto: A.R.F. Books, 1969.

Cummings, E. M. "Coping with Background Anger in Early Childhood." *Child Development,* 1987, *58,* 976–984.

Cummings, E. M., Ballard, M., El-Sheikh, M., and Lake, M. "Resolution and Children's Responses to Interadult Anger." *Developmental Psychology,* 1991, *27,* 462–470.

Cummings, E. M., and Cummings, J. S. "A Process-Oriented Approach to Children's Coping with Adults' Angry Behavior." *Developmental Review,* 1988, *8,* 296–321.

Cummings, E. M., and Davies, P. T. "Maternal Depression and Child Development." [Annual Research Review]. *Journal of Child Psychology and Psychiatry,* 1994a, *35,* 73–112.

Cummings, E. M., and Davies, P. *Children and Marital Conflict: The Impact of Family Dispute and Resolution.* New York: Guilford Press, 1994b.

Cummings, E. M., and Davies, P. T. "Emotional Security as a Regulatory Process in Normal Development and the Development of Psychopathology." *Development and Psychopathology,* 1996, *8,* 123–139.

Cummings, E. M., and Davies, P. T. "Depressed Parents and Family Functioning: Interpersonal Effects and Children's Functioning and Development." In T. Joiner and J. C. Coyne (eds.), *Recent Interpersonal Approaches to Depression.* Washington, D.C.: American Psychological Association, forthcoming.

Cummings, E. M., Davies, P. T., and Simpson, D. S. "Marital Conflict, Gender, and Children's Appraisals and Coping Efficacy as Mediators of Child Adjustment." *Journal of Family Psychology,* 1994, *8,* 141–149.

Cummings, E. M., and El-Sheikh, M. "Children's Coping with Angry Environments: A Process-Oriented Approach." In M. Cummings, A. L. Green, and K. H. Karraker (eds.), *Life-Span Developmental Psychology: Perspectives on Stress and Coping.* Hillsdale, N.J.: Erlbaum, 1991.

Cummings, E. M., Hennessy, K., Rabideau, G., and Cicchetti, D. "Responses of Physically Abused Boys to Interadult Anger Involving Their Mothers." *Development and Psychopathology,* 1994, *6,* 31–41.

Cummings, E. M., Zahn-Waxler, C., and Radke-Yarrow, M. "Young Children's Responses to Expressions of Anger and Affection by Others in the Family." *Child Development,* 1981, *52,* 1274–1282.

Cummings, E. M., Zahn-Waxler, C., and Radke-Yarrow, M. "Developmental Changes in Children's Reactions to Anger in the Home." *Journal of Child Psychology and Psychiatry and Allied Disciplines,* 1984, *25,* 63–74.

Cummings, J. S., Pellegrini, D. S., Notarius, C. I., and Cummings, E. M. "Children's Responses to Angry Adult Behavior as a Function of Marital Distress and History of Interparent Hostility." *Child Development,* 1989, *60,* 1035–1043.

Davies, P. T., and Cummings, E. M. "Marital Conflict and Child Adjustment: An Emotional Security Hypothesis." *Psychological Bulletin*, 1994, *116*, 387–411.

Dodd, D. T., and Roberts, R. L. "Differences Among Adult COA's and Adult nonCOA's on Levels of Self-Esteem, Depression, and Anxiety." *Journal of Addictions and Offender Counseling*, 1994, *14*, 49–56.

Dodge, K. A. "Emotion and Social Information Processing." In J. Garber and K. A. Dodge (eds.), *The Development of Emotion Regulation and Dysregulation*. New York: Cambridge University Press, 1991.

Domenico, D., and Windle, M. "Intrapersonal and Interpersonal Functioning Among Middle-Aged Female Adult Children of Alcoholics." *Journal of Consulting and Clinical Psychology*, 1993, *61*, 659–666.

El-Guebaly, N., and Offord, D. R. "The Offspring of Alcoholics: A Critical Review." *The American Journal of Psychiatry*, 1977, *134*, 357–365.

El-Guebaly, N., West, M., Maticka-Tyndale, E., and Pool, M. "Attachment Among Adult Children of Alcoholics." *Addiction*, 1993, *88*, 1405–1411.

El-Sheikh, M. "Children's Emotional and Physiological Responses to Interadult Angry Behavior: The Role of History of Interparental Hostility." *Journal of Abnormal Child Psychology*, 1994, *22*, 661–678.

El-Sheikh, M. "Children's Responses to Adult-Adult and Mother-Child Arguments: The Role of Parental Marital Conflict and Distress." *Journal of Family Psychology*, 1997, *11*, 165–175.

El-Sheikh, M., Ballard, M., and Cummings, E. M. "Individual Differences in Preschoolers' Physiological and Verbal Responses to Videotaped Angry Interactions." *Journal of Abnormal Child Psychology*, 1994, *22*, 303–320.

El-Sheikh, M., and Cummings, E. M. "Availability of Control and Preschoolers' Response to Interadult Anger." *Behavioral Development*, 1992, *15*, 207–226.

El-Sheikh, M., and Reiter, S. "Children's Responding to Live Interadult Conflict: The Role of Form of Anger Expression." *Journal of Abnormal Child Psychology*, 1996, *24*, 401–415.

Emery, R. E. "Interparental Conflict and the Children of Discord and Divorce." *Psychological Bulletin*, 1982, *92*, 310–330.

Emery, R. E., Weintraub, S., Neale, J. M. "Effects of Marital Discord on the School Behavior of Children of Schizophrenic, Affectively Disordered, and Normal Parents." *Journal of Abnormal Child Psychology*, 1982, *10*, 215–228.

Filstead, W. J., McElfresh, O., and Anderson, C. "Comparing the Family Environments of Alcoholic and 'Normal' Families." *Journal of Alcohol and Drug Education*, 1981, *26*, 24–31.

Fine, E. W., Yudin, L. W., Holmes, J., and Heinemann, S. "Behavioral Disorders in Children with Parental Alcoholism." *Annals of the New York Academy of Sciences*, 1976, *273*, 507–517.

Finn, P. R., and Pihl, R. O. "Men at High Risk for Alcoholism: The Effect of Alcohol on Cardiovascular Response to Unavoidable Shock." *Journal of Abnormal Psychology*, 1987, *96*, 230–236.

Finn, P. R., Zeitouni, N. C., and Pihl, R. O. "Effects of Alcohol on Psychophysiological Hyperreactivity to Nonaversive and Aversive Stimuli in Men at High Risk for Alcoholism." *Journal of Abnormal Psychology*, 1990, *99*, 79–85.

Fitzgerald, H. E., Zucker, R. A., and Yang, H-Y. "Developmental Systems Theory and Alcoholism: Analyzing Patterns of Variation in High-Risk Families." *Psychology of Addictive Behaviors*, 1995, *9*, 8–22.

Fox, N. A. (ed.). *The Development of Emotion Regulation: Biological and Behavioral Considerations*. Monographs of the Society for Research in Child Development, 1994, *59* (2–3, serial no. 240).

Fukunishi, I., Ichikawa, M., Ichikawa, T., Matsuzawa, K., Fujimura, K., Tabe, T., Iida, Y., and Saito, S. "Alexithymia and Depression in Families with Alcoholics." *Psychopathology*, 1992, *25*, 326–330.

Garber, J., Braafladt, N., and Zeman, J. "The Regulation of Sad Affect: An Information Processing Perspective." In J. Garber and K. A. Dodge (eds.), *The Development of Emotion Regulation and Dysregulation*. New York: Cambridge University Press, 1991.

Giglio, J. J., and Kaufman, E. "The Relationship Between Child and Adult Psychopathology in Children of Alcoholics." *International Journal of the Addictions,* 1990, *25,* 263–290.

Gottman, J. M., and Katz, L. E. "Effects of Marital Discord on Young Children's Peer Interaction and Health." *Developmental Psychology,* 1989, *25,* 373–381.

Grych, J. H., and Fincham, F. D. "Marital Conflict and Children's Adjustment: A Cognitive-Contextual Framework." *Psychological Bulletin,* 1990, *108,* 267–290.

Grych, J. H., and Fincham, F. D. "Children's Appraisals of Marital Conflict: Initial Investigations of the Cognitive-Contextual Framework." *Child Development,* 1993, *64,* 215–230.

Hanson, G., and Liber, G. "A Model for the Treatment of Adolescent Children of Alcoholics." *Alcoholism Treatment Quarterly,* 1989, *6,* 53–69.

Havey, J. M., and Dodd, D. K. "Environmental and Personality Differences Between Children of Alcoholics and Their Peers." *Journal of Drug Education,* 1992, *22,* 215–222.

Hennessy, K. D., Rabideau, G. J., Cicchetti, D., and Cummings, E. M. "Responses of Physically Abused and Nonabused Children to Different Forms of Interadult Anger." *Child Development,* 1994, *65,* 815–828.

Heyman, R. E., O'Leary, K. D., and Jouriles, E. N. "Alcohol and Aggressive Personality Styles: Potentiators of Serious Physical Aggression Against Wives?" *Journal of Family Psychology,* 1995, *9,* 44–57.

Hughes, H. "Psychological and Behavioral Correlates of Family Violence in Child Witnesses and Victims." *American Journal of Orthopsychiatry,* 1988, *6,* 103.

Hyphantis, T., Koutras, V., Liakos, A., and Marselos, M. "Alcohol and Drug Use, Family Situation and School Performance in Adolescent Children of Alcoholics." *The International Journal of Social Psychiatry,* 1991, *37,* 35–42.

Jacob, T., and Krahn, G. L. "Marital Interactions of Alcoholic Couples: Comparison with Depressed and Nondistressed Couples." *Journal of Consulting and Clinical Psychology,* 1988, *56,* 73–79.

Jacob, T., and Leonard, K. "Psychosocial Functioning in Children of Alcoholic Fathers, Depressed Fathers, and Control Fathers." *Journal of Studies on Alcohol,* 1986, *47,* 373–380.

Jarmas, A. L., and Kazak, A. E. "Young Adult Children of Alcoholic Fathers: Depressive Experiences, Coping Styles, and Family Systems." *Consulting and Clinical Psychology,* 1992, *60,* 244–251.

Jenkins, J. M., and Smith, M. A. "Marital Disharmony and Children's Behavior Problems: Aspects of a Poor Marriage That Affect Children Adversely." *Journal of Child Psychology and Psychiatry,* 1991, *32,* 793–810.

Jouriles, E. N., Barling, J., and O'Leary, K. D. "Predicting Child Behavior Problems in Maritally Violent Families." *Journal of Abnormal Child Psychology,* 1987, *15,* 165–173.

Jouriles, E. N., and Norwood, W. D. "Physical Aggression Toward Boys and Girls in Families Characterized by the Battering of Women." *Journal of Family Psychology,* 1995, *9,* 69–78.

Kerr, A. S., and Hill, E. W. "An Exploratory Study Comparing ACOA's to Non-ACOA's on Family of Origin Relationships." *Australian Journal of Marriage and Family,* 1992, *13,* 24–33.

Klaczynski, P. A., and Cummings, E. M. "Responding to Anger in Aggressive and Nonaggressive Boys: A Research Note." *Journal of Child Psychology and Psychiatry and Allied Disciplines,* 1989, *30,* 309–314.

Lang, A. R., Johnston, C., Pelham, W., and Gelernter, S. "Levels of Adult Alcohol Consumption Induced by Interactions with Child Confederates Exhibiting Normal Versus Externalizing Behaviors." *Journal of Abnormal Psychology,* 1989, *98,* 294–299.

Leonard, K. E., Bromet, E. J., Parkinson, D. K., Day, N. L., and Ryan, C. M. "Patterns of Alcohol Use and Physically Aggressive Behavior in Men." *Journal of Studies on Alcohol,* 1985, *46,* 279–282.

Leonard, K. E., and Senchak, M. "Alcohol and Premarital Aggression Among Newlywed Couples." *Journal of Studies on Alcohol,* 1993, *11,* 96–108.

Levenson, R. W., Oyama, O. N., and Meek, P. S. "Greater Reinforcement from Alcohol for Those at Risk: Parental Risk, Personality Risk, and Sex." *Journal of Abnormal Psychology,* 1987, *96,* 242–253.

Long, N., Slater, E., Forehand, R., and Fauber, R. "Continued High or Reduced Interparental Conflict Following Divorce: Relation to Young Adolescent Adjustment." *Journal of Consulting and Clinical Psychology,* 1988, *56,* 467–469.

Lund, C. A., and Dwyer, S. L. "Predelinquent and Disturbed Adolescents: The Role of Parental Alcoholism." *Currents in Alcoholism,* 1979, *5,* 339–348.

Makepeace, J. M. "Gender Differences in Courtship Violence Victimization." *Family Relations: Journal of Applied Family and Child Studies,* 1986, *35,* 388.

McCloskey, L. A., Figueredo, A. J., and Koss, M. P. "The Effects of Systematic Family Violence on Children's Mental Health." *Child Development,* 1995, *66,* 1239–1261.

McDonald, P. W., and Prachkin, K. M. "The Expression and Perception of Facial Emotion in Alexithymia: A Pilot Study." *Psychosomatic Medicine,* 1990, *52,* 199–210.

McElligatt, K. "Identifying and Treating Children of Alcoholic Parents." [Special Issue: Overstressed Children and Youth.] *Social Work in Education,* 1986, *9,* 55–70.

Moos, R. H., and Billings, A. G. "Children of Alcoholics During the Recovery Process: Alcoholic and Matched Control Families." *Addictive Behaviors,* 1982, *7,* 155–163.

Moos, R. H., and Moos, B. S. "The Process of Recovery from Alcoholism: III. Comparing Functioning in Families of Alcoholics and Matched Control Families." *Journal of Studies on Alcohol,* 1984, *45,* 111–118.

Nisonoff, L., and Bitman, I. "Spouse Abuse." *Victimology,* 1979, *4,* 131–140.

O'Brien, M., Margolin, G., John, R. S., and Krueger, L. "Mothers' and Sons' Cognitive and Emotional Reactions to Simulated Marital and Family Conflict." *Journal of Consulting and Clinical Psychology,* 1991, *59,* 692–703.

O'Farrell, T. J., and Murphy, C. M. "Marital Violence Before and After Alcoholism Treatment." *Journal of Consulting and Clinical Psychology,* 1995, *63,* 256–262.

Pihl, R. O., Peterson, J., and Finn, P. R. "Inherited Predisposition to Alcoholism: Characteristics of Sons of Male Alcoholics." *Journal of Abnormal Psychology,* 1990, *99,* 291–301.

Plescia-Pikus, M., Long-Suter, E., and Wilson, J. P. "Achievement, Well-Being, Intelligence, and Stress Reaction in Adult Children of Alcoholics." *Psychological Reports,* 1988, *62,* 603–609.

Post, R. M., Weiss, S. R., and Leverich, G. S. "Recurrent Affective Disorder: Roots in Developmental Neurobiology and Illness Progression Based on Changes in Gene Expression." *Development and Psychopathology,* 1994, *6,* 781–813.

Potter-Efron, P., and Potter-Efron, R. "Anger as a Treatment Concern with Alcoholics and Affected Family Members." *Alcoholism Treatment Quarterly,* 1991, *8,* 31–46.

Rolf, J. E., Johnson, J. L., Israel, E., Baldwin, J., and Chandra, A. "Depressive Affect in School-Aged Children of Alcoholics." *British Journal of Addiction,* 1988, *83,* 841–848.

Roosa, M. W., Sandler, I. N., Gehring, M., Beals, J., and Cappo, L. "The Children of Alcoholics Life-Events Schedule: A Stress Scale for Children of Alcohol-Abusing Parents." *Journal of Studies on Alcohol,* 1988, *49,* 422–429.

Rubin, K. H., and Mills, R.S.L. "Conceptualizing Developmental Pathways to Internalizing Disorders in Childhood." *Canadian Journal of Behavioural Science,* 1991, *23,* 300–317.

Rubio-Stipec, M., Bird, H., Canino, G., Bravo, M., and Alegria, M. "Children of Alcoholic Parents in the Community." *Journal of Studies on Alcohol,* 1991, *52,* 78–88.

Sadava, S. W. "Introduction to the Special Issue: Developmental Perspectives on Addictive Behaviors." *Psychology of Addictive Behaviors,* 1995, *9,* 3–7.

Scavnicky-Mylant, M. "The Process of Coping Among Young Adult Children of Alcoholics." *Issues in Mental Health Nursing,* 1990, *11,* 125–139.

Seixas, J. S., and Youcha, G. *Children of Alcoholism: A Survivor's Manual.* New York: Crown, 1985.

Senchak, M., Leonard, K. E., Greene, B. W., and Carroll, A. "Comparisons of Adult Children of Alcoholics, Divorced, and Control Parents in Four Outcome Domains." *Psychology of Addictive Behaviors,* 1995, *9,* 117–156.

Shaw, D. S., and Emery, R. E. "Parental Conflict and Other Correlates of Adjustment in the School-Age Children Whose Parents Have Separated." *Journal of Abnormal Child Psychology,* 1987, *15,* 269–281.

Sher, K. J. *Children of Alcoholics: A Critical Appraisal of Theory and Research.* Chicago: University of Chicago Press, 1991.

Sher, K. J., Walitzer, K. S., Wood, P. K., and Brent, E. E. "Characteristics of Children of Alcoholics: Putative Risk Factors, Substance Use and Abuse, and Psychopathology." *Journal of Abnormal Psychology,* 1991, *100,* 427–448.

Straus, M. A., and Smith, C. "Family Patterns and Child Abuse." In M. A. Straus and R. J. Gelles (eds.), *Physical Violence in American Families.* New Brunswick, N.J.: Transaction, 1990.

Tarter, R. E. "Are There Inherited Behavioral Traits That Predispose to Substance Abuse?" *Journal of Consulting and Clinical Psychology,* 1988, *56,* 189–196.

Tharinger, D. J., and Koranek, M. E. "Children of Alcoholics—At Risk and Unserved: A Review of Research and Service Roles for School Psychologists." *School Psychology Review,* 1988, *17,* 166–191.

Thompson, R. A. "Emotion Regulation: A Theme in Search of Definition." In N. A. Fox (ed.), *The Development of Emotion Regulation: Biological and Behavioral Considerations.* Monographs of the Society for Research in Child Development, 1994, *59,* (2–3, serial no. 240), 25–52.

Thompson, R. A., and Caulkins, S. "The Double-Edged Sword: Emotional Regulation for Children at Risk." *Development and Psychopathology,* 1996, *8,* 163–182.

Tubman, J. G. "A Pilot Study of School-Age Children of Men with Moderate to Severe Alcohol Dependence: Maternal Distress and Child Outcomes." *Journal of Child Psychology and Psychiatry and Allied Disciplines,* 1993, *34,* 729–741.

Walitzer, K. S., and Sher, K. J. "Alcohol Cue Reactivity and Ad Lib Drinking in Young Men at Risk for Alcoholism." *Addictive Behaviors,* 1990, *15,* 29–46.

Wallace, J. "Children of Alcoholics: A Population at Risk." *Alcoholism Treatment Quarterly,* 1987, *4,* 13–30.

Webb, W., Post, P., Robinson, B., and Moreland, L. "Self-Concept, Anxiety, and Knowledge Exhibited by Adult Children of Alcoholics and Adult Children of Nonalcoholics." *Journal of Alcohol and Drug Education,* 1992, *38,* 106–114.

Werner, E. E. "Resilient Offspring of Alcoholics: A Longitudinal Study from Birth to Age Eighteen." *Journal of Studies on Alcohol,* 1986, *47,* 34–40.

West, M. O., and Prinz, R. J. "Parental Alcoholism and Childhood Psychopathology." *Psychological Bulletin,* 1987, *102,* 204–218.

Wierson, M., Forehand, R., and McCombs, A. "The Relationship of Early Adolescent Functioning to Parent-Reported and Adolescent Perceived Interparental Conflict." *Journal of Abnormal Child Psychology,* 1988, *16,* 707–718.

Williams, O. B., and Corrigan, P. W. "The Differential Effects of Parental Alcoholism and Mental Illness on Their Children." *Journal of Clinical Psychology,* 1992, *48,* 406–414.

Wilson, C., and Orford, J. "Children of Alcoholics: Report of a Preliminary Study and Comments on the Literature." *Journal of Studies on Alcohol,* 1978, *39,* 121–142.

Wolfe, D. A. "Child Abusive Parents: An Empirical Review and Analysis." *Psychological Bulletin,* 1985, *97,* 462–487.

Woodside, M. "Research on Children of Alcoholics: Past and Future." *British Journal of Addiction,* 1988, *83,* 785–792.

MONA EL-SHEIKH *is associate professor at Auburn University.*

E. MARK CUMMINGS *is professor at the University of Notre Dame.*

Family emotional expressiveness communicates to children appropriate styles, values, and beliefs about emotions, themselves, and their social world.

How Does Family Emotional Expressiveness Affect Children's Schemas?

Julie C. Dunsmore, Amy G. Halberstadt

Emotions are powerful. Long before the rise of modern psychological science, emotions were linked to transcendent states of ecstatic clarity and to demonic states of possession, witchcraft, and madness. With the advent of modern psychology, the power of emotions was recognized in the central role they held in explanations of psychopathology; sometimes lack of emotional restraint was seen as a cause of psychopathology, and sometimes emotional release was seen as a treatment for psychopathology (Cicchetti, 1990). We know from contemporary research that emotional expressions are prime communication channels, playing an important role in regulating infants' behaviors (Barrett and Campos, 1987; Campos and Barrett, 1984; Klinnert and others, 1983), children's peer relationships (Sroufe and others, 1984), and marriage quality (Gottman and Levenson, 1986). Emotional states influence allocation of attention (Derryberry and Rothbart, 1984), learning and recall (Gilligan and Bower, 1984), and the tendency to resist temptation (Dienstbier, 1984). Emotions are intimately connected to our cognitions and behaviors. Indeed, theorists have suggested that emotions, integrated with cognitive structures or processes, form the basis of personality (for example, Izard, 1984; Malatesta, 1990; Tomkins, 1995).

This manuscript was prepared while Julie Dunsmore was supported by a NIMH National Research Scientist Postdoctoral Award (no. 5 F32 MH10966). The Department of Psychology at North Carolina State University warmly welcomed her during her postdoctoral fellowship and provided facilities for this work. We are also grateful to John S. Wilson and Karen C. Barrett for their comments on the manuscript.

We believe that emotions also play a powerful role in how we learn to function cognitively in the social world, by influencing our schemas about emotional expression and experience, about our selves, and about the nature of the world. Schemas are cognitive generalizations that organize and guide processing of information in the individual's social experience. (Our definition is based on Markus, 1977.) We are confronted with myriad details in all the social situations of which we are a part. In these situations, we must select which details are important to attend to and which aspects define the situation, and we must select appropriate behavior. We use schemas about the world and ourselves to organize and filter out much of the information in situations so that we are left with a manageable amount that can be recognized and processed—the information we believe to be important. And what we believe to be important is what has emotional significance for us (Costanzo and Fraenkel, 1987; Dunsmore, 1997b).

How do we construct these schemas? Researchers on cognitive representations of the self generally theorize a developing role for prior experience (Higgins, 1987; Lewis, 1987; Markus, 1977; Markus and Cross, 1990). For young children, the family is the central arena in which prior experience occurs. There are many reasons that the family environment is so important for young children: the amount of time spent with family members, the importance of family members in meeting their needs, and the salience that family members have for young children. The family environment therefore plays a primary role in children's construction of self- and world-schemas. And the emotional expressiveness of the family is a critical component of the family environment (Halberstadt, 1986, 1991). Even infants recognize at least some aspects of the emotional expression of their caregivers (Haviland and Lelwica, 1987), and after children learn language, much meaning is conveyed nonverbally. Caregivers' emotional expressions guide children's attention to aspects of themselves and the environment, aiding them in evaluating such aspects (Dunsmore, 1997b; Dunsmore and Halberstadt, 1994). We believe that because children grow up in families, and because emotional expression is an important means of communication with young children, family emotional expressiveness is particularly influential in children's construction of self- and world-schemas.

In this chapter, we first discuss some existing theories that are relevant to how family emotional expressiveness influences children's self- and world-views. Although no one, to our knowledge, has articulated a theory concerning the process by which family emotional expressiveness influences children's schemas, several theorists have proposed models linking family emotional expressiveness to children's views of self and others, or to children's development of personality. Each of these distinct models has close conceptual links to our own. Next, we outline our own model of how family emotional expressiveness affects children's schemas. Our model builds on previous theory and identifies specific pathways by which family expressiveness influences children's schemas. We conclude with suggestions for future research.

Theories About How Family Emotional Expressiveness Affects Children's Views of Themselves and the World

Sullivan's Interpersonal Model of Personality Development. The idea that family emotional expressiveness influences how children perceive themselves and their world is not new. While parents may have suspected such an influence for centuries, Sullivan (1940, 1953) was perhaps the first psychologist to articulate a theory proposing that family emotional expressiveness, particularly parental emotional expressiveness, affects children's construction of self- and world-views.

Sullivan proposed that in late infancy, when infants are perceived as educable by their parents, parents become more neutral in their affective tone, reserving expressions of positive emotion for instances when the infant has behaved in a way the parent perceives to be good. Regardless of parents' intentions, their expressions of positive emotion become a reward for the infant. The infant's behaviors that are accompanied by a parent's positive emotional response become part of the infant's "good me" (Sullivan, 1953).

When infants behave in ways that parents perceive to be unsatisfactory—for example, by mouthing a chokable object—parents respond with anxiety that is consistent in intensity with how much they do not want the behavior to happen. Sullivan called this the "grading of anxiety" (1953, p. 159) and considered parents' expressions of anxiety to be the guide for infants' interpretations of the world and of their own behavior. Through repeated experiences of negative parental emotional states and negative reinforcement, infants learn to avoid behaviors that increase their parents' anxiety. Those aspects of the self that elicit parental anxiety become part of the infant's "bad me" (Sullivan, 1953).[1]

Sullivan stated that one function of the self-system is to avoid or decrease the experience of anxiety. Therefore, despite the "essential desirability" (1953, p. 164) of an infant being the "good me," the most important aspect of an infant's self-system is its construction around avoiding behaviors that in the past have resulted in parental anxiety and that in the present are accompanied by warning signs of impending parental anxiety. By avoiding these behaviors, infants are able to maintain a sense of security. Over time, and through repeated experiences, parental positive expressiveness is linked with certain infant behaviors, and parental anxiety is linked with certain other infant behaviors. These repeated experiences are incorporated into a stable "self-system" that is self-maintaining, because experiences that disconfirm the self become difficult to process (Sullivan, 1940). That is, once the self-system is established, experiences that do not "fit" an individual's self-perceptions are difficult to attend to, interpret, and encode into and retrieve from memory, and therefore have little or no impact on the established self-system. Table 3.1 itemizes these key elements of Sullivan's model (along with the four other models and theories discussed in this chapter).

Table 3.1. Theories Linking Family Emotional Expressiveness and Children's Views of Self and World, or Development of Personality

Sullivan's Interpersonal Model of Personality Development	Bowlby's Attachment Model of Personality Development	Malatesta's Theory of Emotional Biases in Personality Development	Dix's Theory of Affective Organization in Parental Socialization	Dunsmore and Halberstadt's Model of Family Emotional Expressiveness in Children's Self- and World-Schema Formation
• Parents' positive emotions function as a reward for the infant's behaviors.	• Presence/absence of attachment figures affects children's *perception of the attachment figures' emotional availability and responsiveness, and their own worthiness.*	• Emotions are discrete entities rather than broad categories such as positive or negative, and have fundamentally different properties and meanings.	• Although parents have greater responsibility for parent-child interactions because of their greater maturity, children and parents transactionally create their relationship.	• Family patterns of emotional expressiveness (both of positive and negative emotions, and of discrete emotions) lead to child expectations for normative emotional experiences and expressions.
• Parents' anxiety functions as negative reinforcement and punishment for the infant's behaviors.	• Children's perceptions of parental availability and responsiveness influence *how well children use emotional communication, and children's emotional responses to situations.*	• People are predisposed toward particular mood states, or patterns of emotional responses, termed "emotional biases."	• Parents feel emotions more intensely in the parent-child interaction when their child's behavior is linked to their goals.	• When others express emotions in a way that is more salient than usual (for example, more intense, longer duration, etc.), the event becomes particularly relevant for children's self- and world-schema formation.
• Self-system constructed around *avoiding behaviors that result in parental anxiety.*	• Presence/absence of attachment figures, and children's perceptions of attachment figures' availability and responsiveness to children's needs, *influence children's working models of self and others.*	• Emotional biases influence perception, behavior, and cognitive processing.	• The emotions that parents and children chronically feel and express depend on parents' abilities to harmonize their goals and those of their children.	• Family attributions about emotional experience and expression
• Once constructed, the self-system is difficult to change, because experiences that do not "fit" are hard to process.		• Children develop emotional biases through everyday social interactions in which they experience some emotions often, in a salient man-	• Parents and children become attuned to the	

ner in which the emotions are linked with the children's self-feeling.	prototypical style of their relationship. • Situations that elicit intense parental emotion are significant in children's learning about themselves and the world.	lead to children's evaluations of their emotional experience. • The match between the child's characteristics, family expressive style and family attributions about emotions, and cultural prototypes for emotional experience and expression lead to children's schema formation and evaluation of their own and others' emotional experiences and expression.

Sullivan's theory provides a compelling argument for the relationship between parental emotional expression in response to particular child behaviors and the child's construction of self. In the section of this chapter that describes our own model, we build on Sullivan's ideas about how family emotional expressiveness may influence which behaviors children think are important in defining themselves and in evaluating others.

Bowlby's Attachment Model of Personality Development. Parental anxiety is the key element for children's development of self-views in Sullivan's model. Bowlby, however, considered parental perceptiveness and responsiveness to be primary in children's development of working models of self and others (Bowlby, 1969, 1980). Key elements of this model are itemized in Table 3.1 and described in the following paragraphs.

Bowlby proposed that individuals' working models of others are based on the individuals' perceptions of the availability and responsiveness of their attachment figures. Individuals' working models of self are based on their perceptions of how attention-worthy and acceptable they are to their attachment figures. Like Sullivan, Bowlby viewed these perceptions as being built over time, in repeated experiences with nurturing others. These working models of self and others combine to influence how likely an individual is to respond with fear to uncertain situations. For example, if individuals perceive that they are unacceptable to their attachment figures, they might think that even if attachment figures are available they will not respond if needed. That view would make individuals more likely to feel vulnerable in uncertain situations, and more likely to experience fear. Conversely, if individuals perceive that they are acceptable to and worthy of sensitive responsiveness from their attachment figures, and if they perceive attachment figures to be available, they may perceive the attachment figures as able and willing to respond if needed. That would make individuals less likely to feel vulnerable in uncertain situations, and less likely to experience fear (Bowlby, 1980).

In the early years of life, the presence or absence of attachment figures is important in the child's perception of the attachment figures' emotional availability and likelihood of responding to the child's needs. Also important in the child's early years, and increasingly important as the child matures, is the child's prediction of how accessible her attachment figures will be when needed. Bowlby did not suggest that particular parental emotions are influential in children's construction of self- and other-views, but rather that parental emotional expressions that lead to children feeling secure and that do not activate children's fear of abandonment lead to children constructing adaptive working models of self and others.[2]

Further developing Bowlby's attachment theory, Bretherton (1990) emphasizes how caregivers' emotional responsiveness to the child may lead to either an open or a restricted flow of information, including information about emotional experience, between attachment partners and within the child. When the flow of emotional communication between caregivers and infants is open, with mutual acknowledgment of emotional signals, infants will easily be able to elaborate and update their working models of self and other. When the flow of emotional communication between caregivers and infants is restricted, infants will not receive enough meaningful feedback about their emotional communication. They will thus have difficulty developing coherent working models of self and other, and these models will be more difficult to elaborate and update as development progresses. Therefore the emotional communication between caregivers and infants will influence not only children's emotional expressiveness but also the structure and content of their working models of self and other.

Two points are especially important with regard to the formulation of self- and world-schemas. First, Bowlby and Bretherton posit that the quality of the attachment relationship influences both the emotions that children experience in social relationships and their cognitive organization of social relationships. Second, not only parent characteristics but also parents' sensitive attunement and accommodation of their responses to their child, or the "match" between parent and child, are important in the quality of the attachment relationship.

Malatesta's Theory of Emotional Biases in Personality Development. Whereas Sullivan and Bowlby discuss emotions as broad categories (for example, positive emotions versus anxiety), Malatesta (1990) considers emotions to be discrete entities with fundamentally different properties. Thus, different emotions, though they may have the same valence, may have different patterns of meaning.

Malatesta (1990) proposes that through repeated experiences people become predisposed toward particular mood states, or patterns of emotional response. These predispositions, which Malatesta terms *emotional biases,* influence perception, behavior, and cognitive processing of information, and therefore determine the individual's phenomenological world. Emotional biases develop through everyday social interactions, through repetitive experiences in which children experience some emotions often, in a salient manner that is central in experience, and in which these emotions become linked with the children's self-feeling. Children learn to assign meaning to their emotional experiences, and emotional biases become incorporated into their personalities, influencing how they perceive the world and choose social behaviors.

We agree with Malatesta's emphasis on the importance of examining the different meanings of discrete emotions. We discuss these meanings in the next major section in connection with family attributions about emotional expression. Highlights of Malatesta's model are itemized in Table 3.1.

Dix's Theory of Affective Organization in Parental Socialization. Like Malatesta, Dix (1991) takes a more discrete view of emotions and considers the particular type of emotion experienced and expressed to be important. Dix notes that parents feel emotions more intensely in parent-child interactions when their children's behavior is more closely linked to the parents' goals, and that the particular emotions (for example, happiness, sadness, anger) that parents experience in these interactions depend on how compatible their goals are with the goals of their children. Therefore the emotions that parents and children will chronically feel—and express—depend on parents' abilities to harmonize their goals and those of their children.

To illustrate these concepts, imagine an interaction in which a child grabs a toy from a playmate and a parent becomes angry at the child. The child's short-term goal is to get the toy. The parent may have the long-term goal of raising a prosocial child, and the child's behavior of grabbing the toy may activate the parent's anxiety about the possibility of not attaining that long-term goal. Thus the parent's anger not only communicates displeasure about the behavior to the child but also tells the child that the behavior was important to the parent. One way this parent could bring his or her long-term goal of raising a prosocial child closer to the child's short-term goal of getting to play with fun toys would be to help the child learn age-appropriate methods of negotiating with peers. Another way the parent could harmonize parental and child goals might be to adjust expectations for and definitions of prosocial behavior in the child.

Through repeated experiences with each other across situations, parents and children become attuned to the prototypical style of their relationship, and to the prototypical situations in which that style is going to be different. "Over time, parents and children develop shared representations of events, stable conceptions of each other, and interdependent behavioral dispositions that determine the affective patterning characteristic of their relationship" (Dix, 1991, p. 7). When parents are able to harmonize their own and their children's goals, parent-child interactions will be marked by positive emotional expressions more often than by negative emotional expressions. This positivity will influence children's views of the relative positivity of the world, of their parents, and of themselves. The particular situations that elicit intense parental emotion will aid children in learning to characterize situations, their parents, and themselves. Thus parental emotional expressions will influence children's world-views, self-views, and views about the role of emotion in the parent-child relationship. We have listed the central points of Dix's model in Table 3.1.

Summary. Like Sullivan, Dix emphasizes the role of parental expression of emotion in activating similar emotions in children, and in calling the children's attention to certain behaviors in the children's construction of self- and world-views. Like Bowlby, Dix emphasizes the importance of parental accommodation to children's needs in children's construction of self- and other-views. And like Malatesta, Dix emphasizes the importance of examining the meaning of discrete emotions and particular emotion-situation linkages in children's construction of their phenomenological view of the world.

These four theorists propose the link between parental emotional expressions/parental socialization and children's construction of self- and world-views. Sullivan looks to parental anxiety as the guide to children for behaviors to avoid, and to the absence of negative parental emotion as a guide for acceptable behaviors; these experiences coalesce into internal images or constructs, the "bad" and "good" me's. Bowlby cites the role of parental positive responsiveness to infants' needs in their feeling of how trustworthy the world is and how worthy of care they are. In turn, these central images of self and other form the core of more elaborate internal models of self and other as the child grows. Malatesta discusses the repetitive experience of particular emotions or patterns of emotion in children's development of emotional predispositions that influence their social perceptions and behaviors. Dix notes that different parental emotions convey different messages to children about the acceptability of their behavior, but all parental emotions tell children that their behavior was important to the parents. All four theorists agree that parental emotional expression gives children information about who they are and what the world is like.

We agree with these theorists that family emotional expression is key to children's formation of self- and world-schemas. Given this theoretical groundwork, the mechanisms by which family emotional expression influences children's formation of schemas now need to be specified. We think that family emotional expressiveness influences children's formation of schemas largely by communicating to children the importance and meaning of emotional expressions in social interactions. In this way, children form schemas about emotional experience and expression, and through repeated linkages of emotional expressiveness with particular behaviors and situations children form schemas about themselves and about the social world. In the next section we outline our model of how family emotional expressiveness influences children's schemas about emotional expression and experience, about themselves, and about their world.

Our Model of How Family Emotional Expressiveness Affects Children's Formation of Schemas

As shown in Figure 3.1, we believe there are four factors of importance in the relationship between family emotional expressiveness and children's schemas: (1) the family's typical pattern of emotional expressiveness; (2) the family's attributions about emotional expressiveness; (3) child factors, such as gender and temperament; and (4) the cultural context in which the family is situated. We propose that these factors interact in complex ways to influence children's schema formation; however, for the sake of clarity we discuss each factor separately, and touch on interactions only briefly.

The Typical Pattern of Emotional Expressiveness in the Family. Family emotional expressive styles may differ in many ways. At the most general level, the overall frequency, intensity, and duration of positive and negative emotional expressiveness in the family is important in the child's formation of schemas about emotionality, about expressiveness, about self, and about the world. (See Halberstadt, Crisp, and Eaton, forthcoming, for a discussion of other relevant dimensions of typicality in emotional expressiveness.) It is important to note that positive and negative emotional expressiveness can be related, but they can also be independent (see, for example, Cassidy, Parke, Butkovsky, and Braungart, 1992; Gross and John, 1995; Halberstadt and

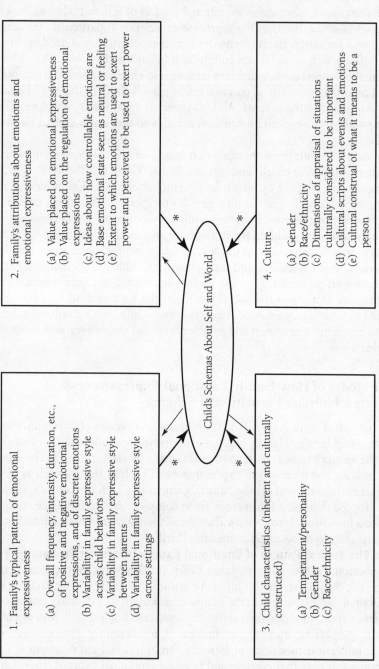

Figure 3.1. How Family Emotional Expressiveness Might Influence Children's Formation of Schemas

1. Family's typical pattern of emotional expressiveness

   (a) Overall frequency, intensity, duration, etc., of positive and negative emotional expressions, and of discrete emotions
   (b) Variability in family expressive style across child behaviors
   (c) Variability in family expressive style between parents
   (d) Variability in family expressive style across settings

2. Family's attributions about emotions and emotional expressiveness

   (a) Value placed on emotional expressiveness
   (b) Value placed on the regulation of emotional expressions
   (c) Ideas about how controllable emotions are
   (d) Base emotional state seen as neutral or feeling
   (e) Extent to which emotions are used to exert power and perceived to be used to exert power

Child's Schemas About Self and World

3. Child characteristics (inherent and culturally constructed)

   (a) Temperament/personality
   (b) Gender
   (c) Race/ethnicity

4. Culture

   (a) Gender
   (b) Race/ethnicity
   (c) Dimensions of appraisal of situations culturally considered to be important
   (d) Cultural scripts about events and emotions
   (e) Cultural construal of what it means to be a person

* These four factors are highly interactive with one another; the degree of match between child, family, and culture is important in children's formation of schemas.

others, 1995). Therefore, a family could be high in positive expressiveness and low in negative expressiveness, or vice versa, or low in both types of expressiveness or high in both types of expressiveness. Families may also vary in their expression of particular emotions; for example, a family could be highly expressive of anger, yet not very expressive of sadness.

We posit that the typicality of family emotional expression has an impact on children's developing schemas in two ways. First, children's schemas about emotional expressiveness are influenced by the typical pattern of emotional expressiveness in their families. Children develop general expectations regarding the basic style of emotional expression and come to have a basic understanding of the world as expressive or nonexpressive. For example, when a family has a high frequency of positive emotional expressiveness, the child comes to expect frequent positive expressiveness; when a family has a high frequency of negative emotional expression, the child comes to expect frequent negative expressiveness. This is not necessarily good or bad, because in a high positive expressive family, positive expression may come to have less meaning in that it is normative.[3] High negative emotional expressiveness might operate similarly, with negative expression coming to have less meaning in a high negative expressive family because it is normative.[4]

This suggests the second kind of impact of the family's typical pattern of emotional expression. When family emotional expressions increase (or decrease) in frequency, intensity, or duration, or change in affective tone or predictability, children have new information to add to their schemas about events and meanings in the world. We believe that changes from the base style of expression, precisely because of their nonnormative nature, become salient to the growing child and are highly invested with meaning about current events and relationships (Costanzo and Fraenkel, 1987). These emotional expressions at levels "above" the typical family style will be especially salient to children, and highlight for them behaviors and situations that are important for defining who they are and what the world is like. In short, the family's *atypical* emotional expressions are crucial in children's formation of schemas about themselves and the social world.

Thus children from less positively expressive families might gather or impute more meaning from positive emotional expressions than would children from more positively expressive families, because the children's expectations for normal expressiveness are different. For example, children who rarely receive highly positive emotional feedback from their parents might be exquisitely sensitive to the situations in which their parents do express positive emotions; they might seek out those situations, and they might learn to define situations and their own behavior in terms of how likely they are to elicit positive emotional expressions from their parents. Children who are quite accustomed to receiving positive emotional feedback from their parents, conversely, might not find the likelihood of eliciting positive emotional expressions from parents to be an effective way of defining situations or their own behaviors. These schemas about defining social situations may carry over into other relationships, so that children from less positively expressive families may also gather or impute more meaning from peers' positive emotional expressions and therefore have different ways of understanding peers' emotional communications and of defining friendship than do children from more positively expressive families. Likewise, children from less negatively expressive families may gather or impute more meaning from a negative expression than the expressor intended.

As children mature and gain experience in contexts outside the family, they often come into contact with people who have different expressive styles from their family. Inevitably their schemas about the meanings of expressiveness are challenged as they try to make sense of ongoing social interactions with diverse others. This may be very difficult, especially initially, when children and adolescents may have only one general model and/or an inflexible sense of the "right" or "wrong" way to do things. This challenge may be particularly acute for children who lack the more cognitively sophisticated ability to take into account multiple perspectives. One developmental task for children, then, is to learn to develop alternative models of emotional expressiveness in varying types of social interactions.

Naturally, within most families emotional expressiveness is not a monolithic construct. First, there is variability in emotional expressiveness between parents (Halberstadt and others, 1995). Parents can vary from having quite similar styles to having very different styles of emotional expressiveness. What happens when parents' expressive styles do not match? One outcome could be that children gain experience with a greater range of expressiveness, and therefore may be able to accommodate more variation in general expressiveness in their schemas and adjust more readily when confronted with peers with different expressive styles. This may happen because children will have acquired (1) knowledge about the variability of emotional expression, (2) acceptance of that variability, (3) willingness to work at interpreting emotional expression, and (4) some skill in interpreting emotional expression. It could also be that the parent who is the primary caretaker has a more influential expressive style, or that because of gender-role identification children are more influenced by the expressive style of their same-sex parent. As we discuss in the next section, the family's attributions about expressiveness may interact to make one parent's style more influential on the child, as when the family labels one parent's expressive style as appropriate and the other's as inappropriate. Both parents' emotional expression styles convey meaning to the child; the particular meaning conveyed may depend on factors such as the family's attributions about emotions, gender role socialization, and so on.

Second, family emotional expressiveness may vary across settings. Some families may show a great deal of reserve and decorum in public settings and become only slightly more expressive when at home; some families are highly expressive at home and become only slightly less so in public; and other families may completely change expressive styles across settings. The extent of variability across settings communicates to children context-specific rules for appropriate behavior. It also exposes them to a greater or lesser degree of emotional variation, leading to more or less elaborate schemas about the world and about emotionality and expressiveness. Finally, the extent of variability in family emotional expressiveness across settings may convey to children the family's attitudes about and sensitivity toward different social relationships.

Third, families have different patterns of responsiveness to different behaviors and situations. For example, some families may respond with a great deal of pride and excitement to a child's academic accomplishments, or with a great deal of anger or sadness to a child's academic failures, while other families do not respond very much to a child's academic behaviors but show high levels of emotional expression when a child behaves prosocially or antisocially (Dunsmore, 1997b). Different families value different things, and behaviors that relate to a family's values will be responded to at levels above the family's background level of typical emotional expressiveness (as when a low positive expressive family responds with intense delight to a child's achievement), or they will be responded to emotionally in ways that are different from the family's typical pattern of emotional expressiveness (as when a family that usually does not express emotions for an extended period goes on and on with delight about a child's prosocial behavior, such as sharing a toy). Again, we believe that these behaviorally specific expressions of emotion, which are communicated in a different way than usual, are highly meaningful to children. These distinctive instances of emotional expression convey not only which behaviors families approve and disapprove of, but also which of the children's behaviors are important in defining who they are as they construct their self-schemas (Dunsmore, 1997b).

The Family's Attributions About Emotional Expressiveness. Families make many attributions, either explicitly or implicitly, about emotional expressiveness. These attributions relate to (1) the value of emotions and emotional expressions, (2) beliefs about and values for regulation of emotions and emotional expressions, (3) emotional base states, and (4) use of power through emotional expressiveness. Attributions about emotional expressiveness contribute to the relationship between family emotional expressiveness and children's formation of schemas.

The Value Placed on Experiencing and Expressing Emotions. Families vary in how they value emotional expressiveness. For example, the first author of this chapter (Dunsmore) comes from a family that views emotional expressiveness, whether positive or negative, quite negatively. In her family, expressing emotions intensely is seen as impolite at best and extremely aggressive and inappropriate at worst. Not coincidentally, her family is in general quite low in emotional expressiveness. The second author (Halberstadt) comes from a family that is highly accepting of emotional expressiveness. In her family, expressing emotions intensely when they are felt intensely, while not always enjoyable, is seen as a necessary aspect of social relationships and of self-discovery. Again, not coincidentally, her family is quite high in emotional expressiveness.[5] In our cases, positive and negative expressiveness are treated similarly (both are devalued in Dunsmore's family and both are accepted in Halberstadt's family), but other families may have complex valuing of expressiveness based on the particular emotions represented. Depending on children's temperamental tendencies to be more or less emotionally reactive, the value that families place on experiencing and expressing emotions may either confirm or challenge children's inner experience. Challenges to children's emotional experience may result in children feeling ambivalence about their own emotional experience and expression. Such ambivalence could be felt by highly emotionally reactive children struggling to meet the standards set by low-expressive families that devalue emotions, or by children who are not very emotionally reactive and wish they could share in the intense emotional expressions of their highly expressive families (King and Emmons, 1991). Therefore, the family's values for expressiveness will influence children's schema formation as children work to understand the meaning of their own and others' emotional experiences and expression. Family valuing of expressiveness may affect children's evaluations of themselves as appropriate or inappropriate experiencers or expressors of emotion, their evaluations of others' emotional expressions, their tendency to express certain emotions, and even their likelihood of experiencing certain emotions (Burrowes and Halberstadt, 1987; Halberstadt, 1984, 1986; Halberstadt, Fox, and Jones, 1993).

   Beliefs About and Value Placed on the Regulation of Emotional Expressiveness. Families also have different beliefs about and values for the regulation of emotional expressiveness. For example, some families believe that any felt emotion can be "hidden," whereas others believe that when an emotion is felt it will eventually have to "come out." Families that believe in the regulation of expressiveness may vary in their beliefs about when and how regulatory skill develops, just as cultures do: the Utku and the Javanese do not emphasize much emotional or expressive control until toddlerhood at the earliest, whereas the Gusii and the Americans begin emotional socialization early in infancy (see Halberstadt, 1991 for a review; see also Briggs, 1970; Dixon, Tronick, Keefer, and Brazelton, 1981; Geertz, 1959).

   We think that it is likely that members of low-expressive families who value low expressiveness will tend to believe that they and their children can attain the goal of controlling emotional expressions.[6] For high-expressive families, two possibilities exist. Expressiveness may be seen as uncontrollable, and thus unavoidable (not valued); alternatively, expressiveness may be seen as controllable and valuable. Family attributions about the controllability and the value of regulating expression and experience of emotions will influence children's interpretations of their own emotional experience and expression, thereby influencing the formation of their self-schemas; and these attributions will influence children's interpretations of others' emotional expression, thereby influencing the formation of their world-schemas. For example, children who belong to families that believe that emotional experience and expression are uncontrollable may find adult expressions of anger, or even their own experiences of anger, to be threatening and frightening. Children who belong to families that believe that emotional experience and expression can and should be controlled might find others' expressions of anger to be contemptible, and their own experiences of anger to be shameful, because they are evidence of loss of control. And children who belong to families that value emotional experience and expression might appreciate the freedom to engage fully in their own anger and to have their feelings and their power acknowledged by family members.

Emotional Base States. A third kind of attribution about emotional experience that may differ across families is whether the base state of an individual is seen as being emotionally neutral or as encompassing some feeling state. Some families may infer that people are emotionally neutral unless something happens to make them feel happy (or sad, or mad, and so on). Or they may believe that people have some feeling state (such as happiness or sadness or anger and so on) unless something happens either to intensify that feeling state or to change it to something else. Again, the family's attributions about base emotional states will influence children's interpretations of their own emotional experience and of the emotional expressions of others, and thereby influence their formation of self- and world-schemas.

Emotional Expression as a Power Play. Finally, the extent to which emotional expressions are used to exert power differs across families, and may differ in particular relationships within families. For example, some families explicitly use negative emotions to discipline children, as when a parent says to a child, "You make me unhappy (or angry, or sad, and so on) when you do that" (Dunsmore, 1997a). Similarly, positive emotions such as pride or happiness may be deliberately withheld in an effort to control a family member. In families with domestic violence, displays of anger by the batterer are often used as power maneuvers (Tifft, 1993). Also, perceptions about the extent to which emotional expressions are used to exert power in relationships differ across families. An example is parental attributions about their children's night waking. Some parents perceive children's crying in the middle of the night as a manipulative ploy to get the parent to come, while other parents perceive the crying as an expression of a need. (Of course, parents' perceptions will be influenced by the age and developmental stage of the child and by specific circumstances, such as the child being ill.) These attributions will determine the extent to which the concept of emotional expression as a power play is represented in children's self- and world-schemas.

Child Characteristics. A third set of factors in the relationship between family emotional expressiveness and child schema formation includes characteristics of the child. In particular, we think that temperament and gender play important roles in how family emotional expressiveness influences children's formation of schemas.[7]

There may be different relationships between family emotional expressiveness and children's formation of schemas according to the child's temperament. For example, easily distracted children may feel overwhelmed by the plethora of emotional expressions in highly expressive families; the many emotional signals might distract them from effectively processing any one signal

As a consequence, these children might develop less elaborate schemas than would less distractable children in highly expressive families. As another example, highly active children in low-expressive families might have difficulty gathering information with which to organize their own experience; and slower-moving, more watchful children might have greater success in low-expressive families. These examples illustrate mismatches between child temperament and the family's typical emotional expressiveness style; however, the same kinds of mismatches could occur between the child's temperament and family attributions about emotional expression. Furthermore, when child temperament fits poorly with family expressive style, children might come to be labeled (by themselves or their families) as odd or different. Although this could have positive consequences, depending on the family's attributions about emotions, it is more likely that such children would feel alienated and less accepted by their families.

Child gender may also affect the relationship between family emotional expressiveness and children's formation of schemas. In middle-class white families, cultural expectations for emotional expression tend to decrease boys' crying and expressions of sadness and increase girls' polite expressions while decreasing their negative-dominant emotional expression (see Brody and Hall, 1993, and Halberstadt, 1991, for reviews). Additionally, gender-role identification may lead girls to be more attuned to the emotional expressions of the female members of their family, and boys to be more attuned to the emotional expressions of the male members of their family. Families also may have different attributions for emotional expressions when expressed by girls or women than when expressed by boys or men.

Child characteristics can in turn affect family expressiveness. For example, parents may learn to be careful not to shout or laugh loudly because it upsets their highly sensitive infant. Enhancement of family expressiveness due to child characteristics may also occur: parents of Down's Syndrome infants may express emotions in an exaggerated fashion in order to elicit smiles from their less emotionally responsive infants (Cicchetti, 1990). In white families, child gender may also affect family expressiveness; several studies suggest that parents may be more emotionally expressive with girls than with boys (see Halberstadt, 1991, for a review).

Cultural Context. The cultural and historical contexts in which the family is situated influence typical patterns of family emotional expressiveness. Research on display rules across cultures (and classes) illustrates that different emotions may be more likely to be displayed in particular cultures (and classes) (Halberstadt, 1991). Furthermore, there are indications that particular emotions may be more likely to be experienced in some cultures than in others (Markus and Kitayama, 1991, 1994). The dimensions that are considered important in one's culture in evaluating the emotional impact of a situation, cultural scripts about the meanings of events and the ways in which emotions are experienced, and cultural understandings of what it means to be a person will all influence how individuals experience and express emotions:

which emotions, in which situations, and with what degree of comfort with the emotions (Ellsworth, 1994; Frijda and Mesquita, 1994; Markus and Kitayama, 1994). Indeed, cultural constructions of emotion will affect whether an individual perceives emotions to be important aspects of situations at all; Potter (1988) has reported that the Chinese believe that emotions are irrelevant in social interaction.[8]

Of course, families will vary in the extent to which their emotional expressivity and attitudes about emotional expressivity match the prototype for their culture. Even when family practices differ quite a bit from cultural practices, children learn the cultural framework about emotional experience and expression. Educators play an important role in children's lives, imparting assumptions about emotional experience and expression and, through their classroom practices, encouraging some forms of emotional experience and expression and discouraging others (Hyson, 1994; Markus and Kitayama, 1994). Entertainment venues, such as film, also convey cultural prototypes for emotional experience and expression (Denzin, 1990). And perhaps most important, in everyday social interactions with others who are part of the culture, children learn what are considered appropriate and inappropriate ways of expressing and experiencing emotions.

The match between the cultural context and family expressive styles and attributions about emotions will have an impact on the meaning to children of their families' expressiveness and their own experience of emotion. For example, suppose a highly emotionally reactive child is part of a highly expressive family that values emotional expressiveness. If this family is part of a highly expressive culture, such a child might have a relatively easy time recognizing and accepting the emotional expressive styles of peers and accommodating her or his expressive style to various settings. However, if this family is part of a low expressive culture that emphasizes regulation of emotional expressiveness, the child might have a difficult time learning to interpret her or his social interactions with peers. Such a child might need to learn alternative expressive styles for various settings early in order to function socially, in school and in peer groups, and this child's positive sense of self might be challenged as she or he struggles to regulate emotion experience and expression to levels appropriate in that culture.

Families will vary in the extent to which their pattern of emotional expressiveness and their attributions about emotional expressiveness match the prototype for their culture. Because cultures are composed of individual families, cultural prototypes for emotional expressiveness may gradually change as growing numbers of families diverge from the cultural prototype. The interaction among family emotional expressive styles, family attributions about emotions, child characteristics, and cultural prototypes for emotional expression will influence the meanings attached to family expressiveness by children, children's repertoires of expressive styles, and children's attributions about their families and about themselves.

Summary. We believe that typical family patterns of emotional expressiveness, family attributions about emotions and emotion expression, child characteristics, and cultural and historical contexts interact to influence children's formation of self- and world-schemas. In particular, these factors combine to determine children's understanding of when emotional expressions are meaningful, which behaviors are important to attend to, and which experiences and expressions of emotion are appropriate. Ultimately what is affected is children's understanding and evaluation of themselves, of the social world, and of their own emotional experience and expression. For example, imagine a highly emotionally responsive child in a low-expressive family that values controlling the experience and expression of emotion. Such a child may come to view emotional experience as something to be afraid of, something that might threaten self-control of her or his own behavior. Alternatively, the same child in a high-expressive family that values expressiveness may come to view emotional experience as something to enjoy, something that enhances relationships with others. Similarly, some children may come to view their emotions as impeding their ability to think rationally, while other children may view their emotions as enhancing thought. Some children may come to view emotional experience and expression as weakness, while other children may view emotional experience and expression as strength.

Finally, the extent to which children "see" emotions and emotion expression at all will be influenced by the combination of their characteristics, their family's typical pattern of expressiveness, their family's attributions about emotion experience and expression, and their culture. If children are temperamentally not very emotionally responsive, come from low-expressive families that consider the base emotional state of people to be neutral, and are part of a culture that considers emotions to be irrelevant in social life, these children may not consider emotional experience and expression to be salient in any way.

Research Supporting Our Model

We have proposed a relationship between family emotional expressiveness and children's cognitive schemas about themselves, the world, and the nature of affect. What evidence is there for this model? Although we know of no empirical work that directly tests these relationships other than the work we have begun (Dunsmore and Halberstadt, 1994), the rich literature on family emotional expressiveness and a variety of social behaviors is relevant to and supportive of our model.

Very briefly, numerous studies indicate that parental emotional expressiveness has an impact on children's emotional expressiveness (see Halberstadt, 1991; Halberstadt, Fox, and Jones, 1993; and Halberstadt, Crisp, and Eaton, forthcoming, for reviews). It appears that children experience particular levels and styles of expressiveness in their home and then develop ideas about what is appropriate and how they too will express emotion. Also, family emotional expressiveness has an impact on children's understanding of emotion: lower family expressiveness may be associated with young children's initial deficits in recognizing emotional expressions (Camras, and others, 1990; Daly, Abramovitch, and Pliner, 1980), but with greater skill in older adolescents and adults (see Halberstadt, 1991, and Halberstadt, Crisp, and Eaton, forthcoming, for a review of those studies). Greater maternal acknowledgment of and discussion of emotions are also associated with children's understanding of emotion (Dunn, Brown, and Beardsall, 1991; Dunn and others, 1991). Finally, family emotional expressiveness has an impact on a variety of social outcomes for children, including appropriate behavior with and responsiveness to siblings, peers, or strangers, and peer popularity (see Halberstadt and others, 1995, and Halberstadt, Crisp, and Eaton, forthcoming, for reviews; see also Boyum and Parke, 1995; Bronstein and others, 1993; Cassidy, Parke, Butkovsky, and Braungart, 1992; Denham and Grout, 1992; Eisenberg and others, 1991, 1992; Garner, Jones, and Miner, 1994). Family expressiveness styles seem to be implicated in a variety of behaviors in children; their pathways of influence may well involve children's schema development.

Conclusions

In this chapter we have emphasized the role of emotion in the development of children's schemas about themselves and their world. We began with theory, describing four writers whose ideas have emerged from different theoretical backgrounds and who focus on different aspects of the development of the self, yet who nevertheless agree about the importance of family emotional expressiveness and its subsequent impact on children's ideas about themselves and their world.

With the general theoretical claim well established, our work has been to consider the specific pathways by which family emotional expressiveness might influence children's formation of schemas. We have focused on four factors: (1) the family's typical pattern of emotional expressiveness, (2) the family's attributions about emotional expressiveness, (3) factors that the child brings to the family dynamic (whether "inherent" or familially or culturally constructed), and (4) the cultural and historical context in which the family is situated. These factors are of course highly interactive with one another and affected by the match between child and family, and among child, family, and culture.

Of striking importance is a recognition of the complexity of the "big picture." Emotional expressiveness is itself complex, and the family structure as a distinct entity is also complex, as of course is the child who is influenced by and influencing many aspects of family dynamics. Schemas, too, can be exceedingly complex, and most complex of all is the concept of process or development. We have not suggested a timetable for the formation of schemas, but we imagine that the formative years for schema development last well into adolescence, and that both self-schemas and world-schemas are affected by peers as well as family. We also expect that children will understand and interpret their expressive worlds differently as they mature cognitively and socioemotionally. For example, children's ability to distinguish between experience and expression of emotions emerges gradually in the early elementary years, and this ability is necessary for more complex understanding and use of display rules (see, for example, Gnepp and Hess, 1986; Saarni, 1979, 1988; Shennum and Bugental, 1982). Further, family styles can have an impact on the development of this ability: children from high-expressive families that do not emphasize emotional control may understand the distinction between experience and expression later than children from low-expressive families that do emphasize control.

Let us return to the beginning: emotions are powerful. From infancy on, emotions are the foundation of our experience. Emotions regulate our social interactions with others. Emotions tell us what other people think about the world and about their relationships with us. Emotions tell us what we think is important, and how we define ourselves. In our framework, emotions provide the base for the individual schemas we all use to understand ourselves and the world. We believe that investigation of how family emotional expressiveness affects children's schema formation will fruitfully intertwine the study of emotion and of cognition, and provide a better understanding of how we develop constructions of the social world.

Notes

1. Sullivan also discusses the development of the "not me," those aspects of the self that are associated with extremely threatening, disorganizing parental emotions. Because the "not me" is assumed to be important in extremely pathological rather than normal development, we do not discuss it here.

2. Evidence of working models may be found in the substantial empirical evidence documenting a relationship between children's secure maternal attachment and positive, adaptive child outcomes (see, for example, Cicchetti, 1990; Erickson, Sroufe, and Egeland, 1985; Jacobsen, Edelstein, and Hofmann, 1994; Main, Kaplan, and Cassidy, 1985; Wilson, 1995).

3. Evidence that positive emotional expression is more meaningful to children when it is more intense than usual may be found in Dunsmore (1997b); children were more likely to include prosocial behavior as part of their self-schemas only when their mothers expressed more happiness than usual in response to children's prosocial behaviors.

4. Alternatively, children from high negative expressive families might become more sensitized to negative emotional expressions (Cummings, 1994). Or there might be a curvilinear relationship for negative expressiveness so that children whose families are moderately negatively expressive gather less meaning from negative emotional expressions because they are normative, while children from low negative expressive and from extremely high negative expressive families are quite sensitive to negative emotional expressions.

5. These examples also point out that attributions about family expressiveness probably influence, and are influenced by, the family's typical pattern of emotional expressiveness.

6. If families are low expressive, then family members will have had the experience of being able to regulate emotional expression. Because of this experience they are likely to believe that they will be able to regulate emotional expressions in the future as they have in the past, and that their children will be able to regulate emotional expressions as they themselves have.

7. We recognize that temperament and gender may be highly interactive with or largely constructed by family and cultural beliefs and by subsequent action with regard to the individual. We do not intend to imply certainty about the degree to which temperament or gender effects are due to "inherent" aspects of the individual.

8. An example of the sociohistorical context for research on expressiveness is the assumption of Jones (1950, 1960) and Lanzetta and Kleck (1970) that socialization with regard to overt expression of emotionality was always punitive and in the direction of depressing expressiveness. It was not until the 1980s that anyone suggested that parents might work to increase expressiveness in their children (Halberstadt, 1984, 1986; Miller and Sperry, 1987).

References

Barrett, K. C., and Campos, J. J. "Perspectives on Emotional Development II: A Functionalist Approach to Emotions." In J. D. Osofsky (ed.), *Handbook of Infant Development*. (2nd ed.) New York: Wiley, 1987.

Bowlby, J. *Attachment and Loss*, Vol. 1. New York: Basic Books, 1969.

Bowlby, J. *Attachment and Loss*, Vol. 3. New York: Basic Books, 1980.

Boyum, L. A., and Parke, R. D. "The Role of Family Emotional Expressiveness in the Development of Children's Social Competence." *Journal of Marriage and the Family*, 1995, 57, 593–608.

Bretherton, I. "Open Communication and Internal Working Models: Their Role in the Development of Attachment Relationships." In R. A. Thompson (ed.), *Socioemotional Development*. Nebraska Symposium on Motivation, 1988, Vol. 36. Lincoln: University of Nebraska Press, 1990.

Briggs, J. L. *Never in Anger*. Cambridge, Mass.: Harvard University Press, 1970.

Brody, L. R., and Hall, J. A. "Gender and Emotion." In M. Lewis and J. Haviland (eds.), *Handbook of Emotions*. New York: Guilford Press, 1993.

Bronstein, P., Fitzgerald, M., Briones, M., Pieniadz, J., and D'Ari, A. "Family Emotional Expressiveness as a Predictor of Early Adolescent Social and Psychological Adjustment." *Journal of Early Adolescence*, 1993, 13 (4), 448–471.

Burrowes, B. D., and Halberstadt, A. G. "Self- and Family-Expressiveness Styles in the Experience and Expression of Anger." *Journal of Nonverbal Behavior*, 1987, 11, 254–268.

Campos, J. J., and Barrett, K. C. "Toward a New Understanding of Emotions and Their Development." In C. E. Izard, J. Kagan, and R. B. Zajonc (eds.), *Emotions, Cognition, and Behavior*. New York: Cambridge University Press, 1984.

Camras, L. A., Ribordy, S., Hill, J., Martino, S., Sachs, V., Spaccarelli, S., and Stefani, R. "Maternal Facial Behavior and the Recognition and Production of Emotional Expression by Maltreated and Nonmaltreated Children." *Developmental Psychology*, 1990, 26, 304–312.

Cassidy, J., Parke, R. D., Butkovsky, L., and Braungart, J. M. "Family-Peer Connections: The Roles of Emotional Expressiveness Within the Family and Children's Understanding of Emotions." *Child Development*, 1992, 63, 603–618.

Cicchetti, D. "The Organization and Coherence of Socioemotional, Cognitive, and Representational Development: Illustrations Through a Developmental Psychopathology Perspective on Down Syndrome and Child Maltreatment." In R. A. Thompson (ed.), *Socioemotional Development*. Nebraska Symposium on Motivation, 1988, Vol. 36. Lincoln.: University of Nebraska Press, 1990.

Costanzo, P. R., and Fraenkel, P. "Social Influence, Socialization, and the Development of Social Cognition: The Heart of the Matter." In N. Eisenberg (ed.), *Contemporary Topics in Developmental Psychology*. New York: Wiley, 1987.

Cummings, E. M. "Marital Conflict and Children's Functioning." *Social Development*, 1994, 3 (1), 16–36.

Daly, E. M., Abramovitch, R., and Pliner, P. "The Relationship Between Mothers' Encoding and Their Children's Decoding of Facial Expressions of Emotion." *Merrill-Palmer Quarterly*, 1980, 26, 25–33.

Denham, S. A., and Grout, L. "Mothers' Emotional Expressiveness and Coping: Relations with Preschoolers' Social-Emotional Competence." *Genetic, Social, and General Psychology Monographs,* 1992, *118,* 75–101.

Denzin, N. K. "On Understanding Emotion: The Interpretive-Cultural Agenda." In T. D. Kemper (ed.), *Research Agendas in the Sociology of Emotions.* Albany: State University of New York Press, 1990.

Derryberry, D., and Rothbart, M. K. "Emotion, Attention, and Temperament." In C. E. Izard, J. Kagan,. and R. B. Zajonc (eds.), *Emotions, Cognition, and Behavior.* New York: Cambridge University Press, 1984.

Dienstbier, R. A. "The Role of Emotion in Moral Socialization." In C. E. Izard, J. Kagan, and R. B. Zajonc (eds.), *Emotions, Cognition, and Behavior.* New York: Cambridge University Press, 1984.

Dix, T. "The Affective Organization of Parenting: Adaptive and Maladaptive Processes." *Psychological Bulletin,* 1991, *110* (1), 3–25.

Dixon, S., Tronick, E., Keefer, C., and Brazelton, T. B. "Mother-Infant Interaction Among the Gusii of Kenya." In T. M. Field, A. M. Sostek, P. Vietze, and P. H. Liederman (eds.), *Culture and Early Interaction.* Hillsdale, N.J.: Erlbaum, 1981.

Dunn, J., Brown, J., and Beardsall, L. "Family Talk About Feeling States and Children's Later Understanding of Others' Emotions." *Developmental Psychology,* 1991, *27* (3), 448–455.

Dunn, J., Brown, J., Slomkowski, C., Tesla, C., and Youngblade, L. "Young Children's Understanding of Other People's Feelings and Beliefs: Individual Differences and Their Antecedents." *Child Development,* 1991, *62,* 1352–1366.

Dunsmore, J. C. "Maternal Emotion and Use of Control: Gender-Specific Pathways to Children's Self-Schematization." Unpublished data, 1997a.

Dunsmore, J. C. "Mothers' Emotional and Controlling Responses Predict Children's Self-Schemas." Unpublished manuscript, 1997b.

Dunsmore, J. C., and Halberstadt, A. G. "Do Mothers' Emotions Affect Children's Memory?" Grant application to the National Institute of Mental Health for an Individual Postdoctoral National Research Scientist Award, 1994.

Eisenberg, N., Fabes, R. A., Carlo, G., Troyer, D., Speer, A. L., Karbon, M., and Switzer, G. "The Relations of Maternal Practices and Characteristics to Children's Vicarious Emotional Responsiveness." *Child Development,* 1992, *63,* 583–602.

Eisenberg, N., Fabes, R. A., Schaller, M., Miller, P., Carlo, G., Poulin, R., Shea, C., and Shell, R. "Personality and Socialization Correlates of Vicarious Emotional Responding." *Journal of Personality and Social Psychology,* 1991, *61,* 459–470.

Ellsworth, P. C. "Sense, Culture, and Sensibility." In S. Kitayama and H. R. Markus (eds.), *Emotion and Culture: Empirical Studies of Mutual Influence.* Washington, D.C.: American Psychological Association, 1994.

Erickson, M., Sroufe, L., and Egeland, B. "The Relationship Between Quality of Attachment and Behavior Problems in Preschool in a High-Risk Sample." In I. Bretherton and E. Waters (eds.), *Growing Points of Attachment Theory and Research.* Monographs for the Society for Research in Child Development, 1985, *50* (1–2, serial no. 209), 147–166.

Frijda, N. H., and Mesquita, B. "The Social Roles and Functions of Emotions." In S. Kitayama and H. R. Markus (eds.), *Emotion and Culture: Empirical Studies of Mutual Influence.* Washington, D.C.: American Psychological Association, 1994.

Garner, P. W., Jones, D. C., and Miner, J. L. "Social Competence Among Low-Income Preschoolers: Emotion Socialization Practices and Social Cognitive Correlates." *Child Development,* 1994, *65,* 622–637.

Geertz, H. "The Vocabulary of Emotion." *Psychiatry,* 1959, *22,* 225–237.

Gilligan, S. G., and Bower, G. H. "Cognitive Consequences of Emotional Arousal." In C. E. Izard, J. Kagan, and R. B. Zajonc (eds.), *Emotions, Cognition, and Behavior.* New York: Cambridge University Press, 1984.

Gnepp, J., and Hess, D. L. "Children's Understanding of Verbal and Facial Display Rules." *Developmental Psychology,* 1986, *22* (1), 103–108.

Gottman, J. M., and Levenson, R. W. "Assessing the Role of Emotion in Marriage." *Behavioral Assessment,* 1986, *8,* 31–48.

Gross, J. J., and John, O. P. "Facets of Emotional Expressivity: Three Self-Report Factors and Their Correlates." *Personality and Individual Differences,* 1995, *19* (4), 555–568.

Halberstadt, A. G. "Family Expression of Emotion." In C. Z. Malatesta and C. E. Izard (eds.), *Emotion in Adult Development.* Thousand Oaks, Calif.: Sage, 1984.

Halberstadt, A. G. "Family Socialization of Emotional Expression and Nonverbal Communication Styles and Skills." *Journal of Personality and Social Psychology,* 1986, *51* (4), 827–836.

Halberstadt, A. G. "Toward an Ecology of Expressiveness: Family Socialization in Particular and a Model in General." In R. S. Feldman and B. Rim (eds.), *Fundamentals of Nonverbal Behavior.* New York: Cambridge University Press, 1991.

Halberstadt, A. G., Cassidy, J., Stifter, C. A., Parke, R. D., and Fox, N. A. "Self-Expressiveness Within the Family Context: Psychometric Support for a New Measure." *Psychological Assessment,* 1995, *7* (1), 93–103.

Halberstadt, A. G., Crisp, V. W., and Eaton, K. L. "Family Expressiveness: A Retrospective and New Directions for Research." In P. Philippot, R. S. Feldman, and E. Coats (eds.), *Social Context of Nonverbal Behavior.* New York: Cambridge University Press, forthcoming.

Halberstadt, A. G., Fox, N. A., and Jones, N. A. "Do Expressive Mothers Have Expressive Children? The Role of Socialization in Children's Affect Expression." *Social Development,* 1993, *2* (1), 48–65.

Haviland, J. J., and Lelwica, M. "The Induced Affect Response: Ten-Week-Old Infants' Responses to Three Emotion Expressions." *Developmental Psychology,* 1987, *23,* 97–104.

Higgins, E. T. "Self-Discrepancy: A Theory Relating Self and Affect." *Psychological Review,* 1987, *94,* 319–340.

Hyson, M. C. *The Emotional Development of Young Children: Building an Emotion-Centered Curriculum.* New York: Teachers College Press, 1994.

Izard, C. E. "Emotion-Cognition Relationships and Human Development." In C. E. Izard, J. Kagan, and R. B. Zajonc (eds.), *Emotions, Cognition, and Behavior.* New York: Cambridge University Press, 1984.

Jacobsen, T., Edelstein, W., and Hofmann, V. "A Longitudinal Study of the Relation Between Representations of Attachment in Childhood and Cognitive Functioning in Childhood and Adolescence." *Developmental Psychology,* 1994, *30,* 112–124.

Jones, H. E. "The Study of Patterns of Emotional Expression." In M. L. Reymert (ed.), *Feelings and Emotions.* New York: McGraw-Hill, 1950.

Jones, H. E. "The Longitudinal Method in the Study of Personality." In I. Iscoe and H. W. Stevenson (eds.), *Personality Development in Children.* Austin: University of Texas Press, 1960.

King, L. A., and Emmons, R. A. "Psychological, Physical, and Interpersonal Correlates of Emotional Expressiveness, Conflict, and Control." *European Journal of Personality,* 1991, *5,* 131–150.

Klinnert, M., Campos, J., Sorce, J., Emde, R., and Svejda, M. "Emotions as Behavior Regulators: Social Referencing in Infancy." In R. Plutchik and H. Kellerman (eds.), *Emotions in Early Development,* Vol. 2: *The Emotions.* Orlando, Fla.: Academic Press, 1983.

Lanzetta, J. T., and Kleck, R. E. "Encoding and Decoding of Verbal Affect in Humans." *Journal of Personality and Social Psychology,* 1970, *16,* 12–19.

Lewis, M. "Social Development in Infancy and Early Childhood." In J. D. Osofsky (ed.), *Handbook of Infant Development.* New York: Wiley, 1987.

Main, M., Kaplan, N., and Cassidy, J. "Security in Infancy, Childhood, and Adulthood: A Move to the Level of Representation." *Monographs of the Society for Research in Child Development,* 1985, *50,* 66–104.

Malatesta, C. Z. "The Role of Emotions in the Development and Organization of Personality." In R. A. Thompson (ed.), *Socioemotional Development.* Nebraska Symposium on Motivation, 1988, Vol. 36. Lincoln: University of Nebraska Press, 1990.

Markus, H. "Self-Schemas and Processing Information About the Self." *Journal of Personality and Social Psychology,* 1977, *35,* 63–78.

Markus, H., and Cross, S. "The Interpersonal Self." In L. A. Pervin (ed.), *Handbook of Personality: Theory and Research.* New York: Guilford Press, 1990.

Markus, H. R., and Kitayama, S. "Culture and the Self: Implications for Cognition, Emotion, and Motivation." *Psychological Review,* 1991, *98* (2), 224–253.

Markus, H. R., and Kitayama, S. "The Cultural Construction of Self and Emotion: Implications for Social Behavior." In S. Kitayama and H. R. Markus (eds.), *Emotion and Culture: Empirical Studies of Mutual Influence.* Washington, D.C.: American Psychological Association, 1994.

Miller, P., and Sperry, L. L. "The Socialization of Anger and Aggression." *Merrill-Palmer Quarterly,* 1987, *33,* 1–31.

Potter, S. H. "The Cultural Construction of Emotion in Rural Chinese Social Life." *Ethos,* 1988, *16,* 181–208.

Saarni, C. "Children's Understanding of Display Rules for Expressive Behavior." *Developmental Psychology,* 1979, *15,* 424–429.

Saarni, C. "Children's Understanding of the Consequences of Dissemblance of Nonverbal Emotional-Expressive Behavior." *Journal of Nonverbal Behavior,* 1988, *12* (4, part 2), 275–294.

Shennum, W. A., and Bugental, D. B. "The Development of Control Over Affective Expression in Nonverbal Behavior." In R. S. Feldman (ed.), *Development of Nonverbal Behavior in Children.* New York: Springer, 1982.

Sroufe, L. A., Schork, E., Motti, F., Lawroski, N., and LaFrenire, P. "The Role of Affect in Social Competence." In C. E. Izard, J. Kagan, and R. B. Zajonc (eds.), *Emotions, Cognition, and Behavior.* New York: Cambridge University Press, 1984.

Sullivan, H. S. *Conceptions of Modern Psychiatry.* New York: Norton, 1940.

Sullivan, H. S. *The Interpersonal Theory of Psychiatry.* New York: Norton, 1953.

Tifft, L. L. *Battering of Women: The Future of Intervention and the Case for Prevention.* Boulder, Colo.: Westview Press, 1993.

Tomkins, S. S. *Exploring Affect: The Selected Writings of Silvan S. Tomkins* (E. V. Demos, ed.). New York: Cambridge University Press, 1995.

Wilson, J. S. "Attention, Attachment and Motivation in Schizotypy: A Review and Extension of Research with the Continuous Performance Test." Unpublished doctoral dissertation, Department of Psychology: Social and Health Sciences, Duke University, 1995.

JULIE C. DUNSMORE is assistant professor of psychology at Hamilton College, Clinton, New York.

AMY G. HALBERSTADT is associate professor of psychology at North Carolina State University, Raleigh.

Seven postulates regarding the roles of emotion communication in the development of shame and guilt are presented, along with some supportive evidence.

Emotion Communication and the Development of the Social Emotions

Karen Caplovitz Barrett, G. Christina Nelson-Goens

In this chapter we discuss the role of emotion communication in the development of the "social emotions" during infancy and early childhood according to our functionalist perspective, along with some relevant published and unpublished empirical evidence. The focus of the discussion is on the development of shame, pride, and guilt, rather than other social emotions.

It is beyond the scope of this chapter to explicate fully the larger theoretical model of emotional development, of which this topic is a part. For more complete descriptions of this functionalist view of emotions and their development, see Barrett and Campos (1987) or Barrett (forthcoming). For a more complete discussion of emotion communication according to this approach, see Barrett (1993b), and for further discussion of shame and guilt, see Barrett (1995).

Before we begin describing the development of social emotions and the roles of emotion communication in this development, we briefly define our concepts of *social emotions* and *emotion communication,* after which we present postulates concerning the roles of emotion communication in the development of pride, shame, and guilt. Finally, we elaborate each postulate and discuss extant research that is relevant to each, when possible. The discussion of research findings is meant to be illustrative rather than comprehensive and will draw on the published literature as well as on unpublished results from a project-in-progress regarding seventeen-month-olds and their parents.

What Are Social Emotions?

This chapter concerns itself with a class of *emotion families* that we label as *social* and that includes embarrassment/shame, guilt, pride, and envy/jealousy.

NEW DIRECTIONS FOR CHILD DEVELOPMENT, no. 77, Fall 1997 © Jossey-Bass Inc., Publishers

It is important to note that emotions can be divided into categories in many ways. The present concept of emotion families is used to group together emotion processes that share important functions. However, there is nothing sacrosanct about the specific boundaries that are made between families or classes of families, nor even about which distinctions among specific concerns and functions are emphasized (for example, the internal-regulatory function of highlighting and enforcing social standards could be seen as a special case of highlighting goals/concerns). The boundaries for emotion families may be affected by language and culture (Kitayama and Markus, 1994; Menon and Shweder, 1994; Scherer, Walbott, Matsumoto, and Kudoh, 1988), and this is especially true for social emotions (for example, see Menon and Shweder, 1994). For some discussion of cultural variants of social emotions, see Kitayama, Markus, and Matsumoto (1995); Menon and Shweder (1994); Miyake and Yamazaki (1995); or Walbott and Scherer (1995).

The fact that we label guilt, shame, and pride as social emotions should not be taken to imply that other emotions are *asocial*. All emotions serve as social signals to other people and are typically affected by the sociality of the context (see, for example, Barrett, 1993b; Fridlund, 1991). Moreover, all emotions *can* revolve around social concerns. One can be happy to see a friend, sad to see the friend leave, angry because the friend left without saying goodbye, and so on.

However, the social emotions are social in a number of other ways as well, all of which are relevant to the present chapter. Social emotions *always* seem to involve a real or perceived other (or at times the socially constructed self as object; see Mead, 1925). For example, guilt is aroused when someone perceives himself or herself to have harmed a person—usually another, but potentially the self taken as an object (see Barrett, 1995; Baumeister, Stillwell, and Heatherton, 1995). Moreover, there is some evidence that more guilt is experienced when a loved and/or esteemed other is harmed than when a stranger is harmed, and that one is more likely to try purposefully to make loved ones rather than strangers feel guilty (Baumeister, Stillwell, and Heatherton, 1995). Similarly, shame typically involves the perception that someone finds one wanting or deficient (Barrett and Campos, 1987; Lewis, 1971; Stipek, Recchia, and McClintic, 1992); an observing other is perceived, even if only in one's mind. Moreover, social emotions also highlight the importance of social relationships and/or repair them (Barrett and Campos, 1987; Baumeister, Stillwell, and Heatherton, 1995; Lindsay-Hartz, de Rivera, and Mascolo, 1995).

In contrast, one can think of circumstances in which no person, imagined or real, seems to be involved in one's emotions—one is happy when one finds a coin in the coin return of a telephone, sad that one does not have any candy left, angry that one cannot reach the toy one desires. Sociality would be expected to affect the communicative function of these emotions, but lack of a real or imagined observer would not preclude these emotion processes from occurring.

An additional reason that these emotions are considered social emotions is that the concerns of these emotions are believed to be socially constructed. The central concern of the person experiencing shame, guilt, and pride is meeting or failing to meet societal rules or standards. One would not have, much less care about, such standards if one did not live in social groups. Relatedly, these emotions serve societal internal-regulatory functions. Shame, guilt, and pride serve to teach, test, and enforce social standards (see, for example, Ausubel, 1955; Barrett and Campos, 1987; Baumeister, Stillwell, and Heatherton, 1995; Lindsay-Hartz, de Rivera, and Mascolo, 1995).

The behavior-regulatory functions of shame and guilt are social as well. Shame serves to distance the experiencing individual from important others, especially others who can evaluate or are evaluating one. In particular, in shame activated behaviors are aimed at removing the *face* from exposure to others' evaluation. The shameful person avoids looking at others, hides the face, slumps the body, lowers the head, and/or removes himself or herself from contact with others (see, for example, Barrett, 1995; Lewis, 1971; Lewis, 1990; Tangney, 1995). These same behaviors serve social regulatory/social communication functions. The gaze aversion, slumping, hiding, and social withdrawal behaviors communicate deference and submission to others, and indicate that one feels "small," "low," or unworthy in comparison to them.

Guilt serves different functions that are also social. Guilt-relevant behaviors are aimed at repairing the damage caused by the person's wrongdoing and/or at confessing, both of which also help to repair the person's relationship with the person who was harmed (see, for example, Barrett, 1995; Baumeister, Stillwell, and Heatherton, 1995; Ferguson, Stegge, and Damhuis, 1991). Moreover, envy/jealousy, via its social consequences, would seem to provide for equitable distribution of resources for the common good. Thus the term *social emotions* seems to capture what is special about this class of emotions. It also suggests why communication should play an important role in the development of these emotions.

What Is Emotion Communication?

We view emotion communication as synonymous with social regulation by emotion, and operationalize it as systematic changes in another's perceptions, thoughts, feelings, and/or behavior as a function of any or all perceptible aspects of one's emotion, in relation to the context in which it occurs (see Altmann, 1968; Chevalier-Skolnikoff, 1973; Marler, 1965). It is important to recognize that each communication signal is a part of a bidirectional process. One individual starts the process of emotion communication, but by responding to that individual's emotion signals, the *recipient* of the communication is himself or herself likely to be communicating to the other individual and to additional individuals who are present. Each partner shapes and is shaped by the other partner's responses. Moreover, each partner's experiences with the other partner, and with persons or events they construe as similar to those involved in this encounter, play an important role in the communication process.

Emotion communication may or may not be intentional on the part of either partner to the communication. Intentional communication increases in likelihood as the infant becomes older. A particular emotion family has been communicated to the extent that the partner responds in accordance with the function implied by that emotion for that partner in that context. For example, if an adult communicates anger toward a young child or baby after that child scribbles on the wall, the child would be expected to respond with withdrawal and/or appeasement behavior and/or to cease drawing on the wall.

Communication is one function of each emotion process as it evolves, in context. Many elements of the emotion process may have social-regulatory value, including some physiological behaviors (for example, respiration changes or flushing), facial changes, vocalizations, words, instrumental actions, and noninstrumental actions (for example, "nervous" behaviors such as twisting the hair).

This functionalist view, at least in regard to facial movements, is very similar to that of Fridlund (1991); however, Fridlund does not construe facial communication in terms of *emotion* but rather in terms of *social motives*— motives to influence others in particular ways. In the position taken in this chapter, social motives are part and parcel of every emotion process; such motives are one of the three functions that define emotion. Thus the distinction between social motives and emotion is not useful.

Communication and Context. Communication of emotion is always embedded in a context: there are no movements that can be considered clearcut, context-free expressions of emotion, at any period of development. This has implications both for the development of the social emotions and for the *investigation* of the role of emotion communication in the development of the social emotions. Parents and other socializing agents interpret children's emotion communication, and children interpret socializing agents' communication in conjunction with information about ongoing events. A parent's smile after a child has succeeded at a difficult task conveys a very different message than the same parent's smile after the child has failed at that task. There is some evidence of this from our study of seventeen-month-olds: parental smiling in different contexts (for example, after the child succeeded versus after the child violated standards) had very different correlates, both in terms of child reactions and in terms of parental personality dimensions.

To study emotion communication as well, the context must be carefully considered. To understand clearly what functions are being served by particular nonverbal behaviors, one must understand the antecedents, concomitants, and consequents of the responses. The increased attention given in recent years to the development of social emotions in toddlerhood has contributed to increasing skepticism regarding how to "measure" emotion. Whereas some researchers would be content to use decontextualized facial responses to study fear, anger, joy, or other "basic" emotions, most are reluctant to do so to study pride, shame, embarrassment, or guilt. Smiles typically are measured in studies of joy, but they are also measured in studies of pride and embarrassment (see Barrett, Zahn-Waxler, and Cole, 1993; Lewis, Sullivan, Stanger, and Weiss, 1989; Stipek, Recchia, and McClintic, 1992). "Sad" facial movements are sometimes studied in connection with shame (see Geppert, 1986; Stipek, Recchia, and McClintic, 1992). In the context of studies of shame, embarrassment, and pride, it becomes more apparent that decontextualized facial patterns are not clear indicators of specific emotions.

The Relation Between Feeling and Emotion Communication. The model presented in this chapter does not assume that emotion communication necessarily implies emotion feeling, even in earliest infancy. The concept of emotional authenticity has always presented a problem for researchers of emotion. If, as is frequently true, several different measures of emotion conflict (for example, physiological measures suggest emotionality but self-report suggests absence of emotion), researchers have long been concerned with which measure is veridical. According to the present model, both of these responses are elements in the emotion process, and neither is "correct." One may have an emotion process that is devoid of feeling, devoid of a significant change in physiology, and/or devoid of a change in facial movement. Each of these variations would be construed as a different member of the emotion family. Moreover, if a person's face, voice, or body posture communicates a particular emotion family to another person, then one function of that emotion family has been served even if the person who communicated the emotion does not believe that he or she was experiencing that emotion. Nevertheless, although feeling states are not central or even necessary to the emotion process, they can be important regulators of intraindividual and interindividual processes.

Now that we have briefly described our views of social emotions and emotion communication, we describe propositions regarding the roles of emotion communication in the development of the social emotions. There is a paucity of evidence regarding many of these postulates, but ongoing research efforts are beginning to address several of them.

Seven Propositions Regarding the Role of Emotion Communication in the Development of Shame, Pride, and Guilt

1. The emotion communication of parents (and probably other socializing agents) indicates approval or disapproval of children's ongoing behavior, endowing that behavior, in its context, with significance.
2. The emotion communication of children and of their parents (and probably other socializing agents) both is influenced by and helps in establishing a relationship between the children and the parents or socializing agents.
3. Children's emotion communication in the context of success and failure in meeting standards helps parents (and probably other socializing agents) in understanding the children's abilities, needs, interests, and goals, and

indicates the level of difficulty and performance that children consider satisfactory.

4. The emotion communication of parents (and probably other socializing agents) in the context of children's success and failure in meeting standards indicates the level of difficulty and performance that parents (or other socializing agents) consider satisfactory.

5. Children's emotion communication functions to convey to parents (and probably other socializing agents) that children are uncertain about a social rule.

6. Children's emotion communication tells parents (or other socializing agents) that the children understand and care that they have upheld or violated a social standard.

7. Parents' (and probably other socializing agents') *perception* of children's shame, guilt, or pride affects socialization practices even if children's responses would not be construed as shame, guilt, or pride by researchers or theoreticians in the field.

Elaboration and Presentation of Evidence Bearing on the Postulates

1. *The emotion communication of parents (and probably other socializing agents) indicates approval or disapproval of children's ongoing behavior, endowing that behavior, in its context, with significance.* The proposition that emotion communication can indicate approval or disapproval is so intuitively obvious that it is often taken as an assumption in research on discipline. Moreover, when one cares about someone and that person expresses approval or disapproval of one's behavior, it endows that event (behavior in context) with significance (a sense of the relevance of that event to one's well-being in that context). Endowment of social standards with significance is viewed as crucial to the development of shame and pride; if one does not care about standards and rules, and about other people's evaluation of one's behavior, shame and pride should not be manifested, given that key elements of both shame and pride are evaluation with respect to standards, and displays to others in reaction to such evaluation (for more information about processes of endowing events with significance, see Barrett and Campos, 1987). One essential element in the development of shame and pride, thus, is learning to care about a wide array of standards and rules, and about others' evaluation of one's performance relative to them.

Emotional communication around standards, rules, and achievement/mastery in particular may aid in this process of ascribing significance to relevant contexts for shame, pride, and guilt. Standards, rules, and achievement/mastery are all closely related concepts. By standards, we mean some criterion for correct performance, such as completing an entire puzzle. Rules involve prescriptions and proscriptions that define appropriate or desirable behavior, such as "Pick up toys that you drop on the floor" or "Don't touch electrical outlets." By *achievement/mastery* we mean accomplishing some task or goal after exerting some effort toward doing so. For example, a toddler who is just learning to walk has displayed achievement/mastery if she or he toddles across the room to the parent.

Emotion communication often occurs in such contexts. For example, a parent might react with anger and grab a child when the child starts to touch an electrical outlet, or he or she may react with joy and applause when the child completes a tower or when the child smiles after completing the tower. Moreover, research on *social referencing* suggests that by the end of the first year of life, infants are less prone to approach something about which adults communicate negative emotion and more prone to pursue something about which they communicate positive emotion (see, for example, Klinnert and others, 1983; Walden, 1991).

Very little direct information exists regarding the effects of such communication on the development of social emotions, however. Stipek, Recchia, and McClintic (1992) found that although toddlers showed pridelike behavior even when parents did not praise them (in fact, toddlers were more likely to show pride-relevant behavior when they initiated the activity, and parents were more likely to praise success on parent-initiated activities), greater parental praise for children's achievement was associated with children's more frequent positive reactions to achievement *when they were not being praised*. Alessandri and Lewis (1993) did not replicate this finding, but they did find that children's shame responses were associated with parents' increased negative evaluations and decreased positive evaluations.

Pilot data on a small sample of eleven-month-olds and their parents (Barrett, MacPhee, and Sullivan, 1992) indicated, in keeping with speculations by Stipek, Recchia, and McClintic (1992), that parents did not react negatively to their infants' unsuccessful mastery attempts, suggesting that parental reactions to failure could not endow failure with significance at this age. However, additional work with seventeen-month-olds and their parents suggested that by this age parents do react more negatively when children are unsuccessful than when they are successful, and they react more negatively when children violate a social rule (for example, throw blocks) than when they follow a social rule (such as sharing blocks; see Barrett, 1993a). If a child did not already construe the situation negatively, parents' apparent disapproval, as expressed through negative emotion communication (negative facial pattern, negative voice, or negative words, in context), could endow the event with significance, teaching the child to evaluate lack of success and rule violations negatively.

Nevertheless, additional data from the same sample of seventeen-month-olds and their parents suggested that parents' *positive* reactions (positive face, voice, or words, in context) to their children when the children followed rules and succeeded on mastery opportunities that arose during free play (such as putting rings on a ring stack toy) may have more influence on the children's reactions to rule violations and success and failure than parents' negative reactions to children's failure or rule infraction. Correlations among some relevant measures indicated that

Children whose parents displayed more frequent positive reactions when the children followed social rules during free play displayed more guilt-relevant behavior (pointing out and repairing the wrongdoing) when they believed they had broken the experimenter's doll (a completely separate event).

Children whose parents reacted more positively when the children mastered something were themselves more likely to react positively when they mastered something.

Children whose parents reacted more positively when the children mastered something were more likely to react *negatively* when they were *unsuccessful* at something.

Moreover, a canonical correlation between children's and parents' negative reactions to children's lack of success and positive reactions to children's success revealed two canonical variates. The first variate was defined positively by both child variables and by parents' positive reactions to mastery. Thus children's appropriate reactions to success and failure were associated with parents' positive reactions to their success. The second canonical variate was defined positively by children's negative reactions to failure, negatively by children's positive reactions to mastery, and negatively by parents' negative reactions to failure. Thus children who reacted to failure with a larger number of negative responses but to success with fewer positive reactions had parents who were very unlikely to react negatively to their failure. It seems plausible that the parents of such children react less negatively because they can see that their children already endow failure with significance, and they believe that their negative, disapproving reactions would only increase their children's negative reactions.

2. *The emotion communication of children and of their parents (and probably other socializing agents) both is influenced by and helps in establishing a relationship between the children and the parents or socializing agents.* As alluded to earlier, emotion communication typically occurs in the context of a relationship between the participants in the communication process. To the extent that a child and a socializing agent are not connected with one another in a way that is important to the child, the child should be less inclined to heed a communication that the socializing agent originates. Even a role relationship such as "she is an adult, I am a child" may be sufficient to cause a child to heed the communication and endow the standard with significance. However, a relationship in which the child cares deeply about the communicator (for example, a parent) and trusts the communicator would seem more likely to induce the child to endow significance to the events on a long-term basis. Simply stated, if children care about a parent and trust that parent to keep them safe, they are more likely to accept the parent's communication indicating that the standard is significant.

In the literature on child-rearing, a consistent finding is that a warm, reciprocal relationship in which children and parents seem to "meet minds" and interact harmoniously, is associated with children's long-term adherence to standards or rules that are concurrently imposed by the parent or that have already been internalized by the child from past experience (see, for example, Kochanska and Aksan, 1995; Londerville and Main, 1981; Maccoby and Martin, 1983; Parpal and Maccoby, 1985; Rocissano, Slade, and Lynch, 1987; Silverman and Ragusa, 1990). It seems quite possible that one reason that children from such harmonious relationships adhere to parental standards is that such adherence has become significant to them because they care what their parents think. Adhering to parental standards becomes significant via a significant relationship with the parents. Thus a positive relationship between the child and socializing agent is likely to increase the success of that agent's socializing attempts, including those involving emotion communication. Moreover, we think it likely that one important basis for the development of such positive relationships is positive emotion communication between adult and child (see also Izard, 1977).

There is abundant evidence that smiles beget smiles and negativity begets negativity in parent-child interaction (see, for example, Denham, 1989, 1993; Jones and Ragg, 1989; Malatesta and Haviland, 1982; Messinger, 1994; Patterson and Cobb, 1971), and that positive versus negative interaction patterns between parents and their children of a variety of ages are predictive of the positivity of those children's relationships with their parents (see, for example, Gianino and Tronick, 1988; Trevarthen, 1984; Patterson and Cobb, 1971), and even with peers (for example, Denham, Renwick, and Hewes, 1994; Parke and others, 1992). Moreover, as previously mentioned, parents' praise of their toddlers' achievement or mastery is associated with the children's greater tendency to smile in response to achievements for which they were not praised (Stipek, Recchia, and McClintic, 1992). In addition, reciprocated positive emotion communication between parents and their toddlers is associated with toddlers' "internalization of standards," which includes some guilt- and shame-relevant items, as reported by their parents. When accompanied by age and gender, reciprocated positive emotion communication is associated with observed *internalization* ("committed compliance," which involves complying with the parents' command without the parent needing to repeat the directive) (Kochanska and Aksan, 1995). The latter two findings highlight more specifically the importance of positive parent-child emotion communication in the context of socialization of social emotions and internalization of social standards. Moreover, the findings that reciprocity of positive emotion was important and that praise was related to positivity in response to *unpraised achievements* are consistent with the idea that the climate and relationship quality established by praise and positive emotion, rather than simple increase in a response such as smiling or compliance due to positive reinforcement, are important.

3. *Children's emotion communication in the context of success and failure in meeting standards helps parents (and probably other socializing agents) in understanding the children's abilities, needs, interests, and goals, and indicates the level of difficulty and performance that children consider satisfactory.*

4. *The emotion communication of parents (and probably other socializing agents) in the context of children's success and failure in meeting standards indicates the level of difficulty and performance that parents (or other socializing agents) consider satisfactory.*

The general concept that children's emotion communication tells socializing agents about their interests, needs, and goals is not new. Many theorists have suggested that children's smiles indicate to caregivers that the child likes what is going on, and that distress indicates that they do not like what is occurring (see, for example, Izard and Malatesta, 1987; Sroufe, 1979). Moreover, a child's negative emotion upon failure indicates some degree of awareness of the failure, and smiling at success indicates some awareness of succeeding. As a result, socializing agents can empathize with the child, change the task, give suggestions, and so on, if they see the child's distress at failure; or they can praise the child, react positively themselves, or give the child additional similar tasks if the child suggests, by smiling, that he or she is enjoying the successful venture. To our knowledge there is no direct evidence of this process, in which infants or young children communicate their abilities, needs, interests, or goals in a context in which social standards are met or broken and parents respond in accordance with that communication. However, there are some relevant findings.

Stipek, Recchia, and McClintic (1992) found that when toddlers smile following success, they often share these reactions with their parents. However, they did not investigate the degree to which parents were responsive to those communications, nor the degree to which toddlers' reactions varied with difficulty level or other features of the problem that was solved; thus it is not clear whether any kind of standards were being met, or whether specific information about abilities, needs, or goals was being communicated. Similarly, although they noted that parents praised their children's successes, they did not relate this praise to difficulty level or other standards.

Alessandri and Lewis (1993, 1996; see also Lewis, Alessandri, and Sullivan, 1992) have demonstrated that preschoolers react with pridelike responses when they succeed, particularly when they succeed at difficult tasks, and that girls (particularly maltreated girls) display shamelike responses when they fail, especially when they fail on easy tasks. Thus the emotion communication could convey something about the level of performance that children considered satisfactory. Moreover, mothers reacted more positively when preschoolers succeeded, and more negatively when preschoolers failed, and it is possible that their reactions were responsive to the children's reactions.

Reissland (1994) found that parents of toddlers, as well as older toddlers themselves, smiled more when children succeeded at their highest levels of performance than when they succeeded at lower levels of performance. Thus both children's and parents' displays provided potential information about the level of performance deemed satisfactory. However, again, it is not clear to what extent parents' reactions were affected by children's reactions. It seems possible that their reactions were responsive to their children's reactions and/or that they resulted from parents' own beliefs about their children's abilities and/or observation of which of the tasks their children successfully attempted were the hardest.

Finally, recent analyses from our study of seventeen-month-olds addressed the parent and child behaviors that were most probable immediately following the toddlers' success and failure, using sequential analyses (Nelson and Barrett, 1997). Child and parental behavioral consequents that were studied included Duchenne smiles (smiles associated with reports of pleasure in some studies of adults; see, for example, Ekman and Friesen, 1982) non-Duchenne smiles (less commonly associated with pleasure in adults, and associated with embarrassment in at least one study of adults; see Ekman and Friesen, 1982; Keltner and Buswell, 1996), gaze at the other dyad member, and none of the above, following toddlers' success and failure on an easy puzzle and failure on a hard puzzle. Unfortunately, the number of observations of each type of response was not sufficient to perform analyses regarding parent consequents of child responses for success and failure on each type of puzzle. We were able to determine child and parent consequents of only the antecedents "child success on the easy puzzle," "child failure on the easy puzzle," and "child failure on the hard puzzle."

Results indicated that following success on an extremely easy puzzle the most probable response of both parents and children was to *refrain* from smiling or looking at one another, although *children* (but not their parents) were almost as likely to show a Duchenne smile (the difference in incidence of Duchenne smile as a consequent compared with "no response" as a consequent was not significant). In contrast, when toddlers failed on the same easy puzzle, both they and their parents were most likely to respond in some fashion—their *least* likely response was "no response." Children were most likely to look at their parents following failure on the easy task, and there was also a trend for them to display a non-Duchenne smile. Moreover, parents were significantly more likely both to show non-Duchenne smiles and to look at the child than to show "no response" as consequents of children failing on the easy puzzle.

In addition, although the N with sufficient data for the analysis of responses to failure on the hard puzzle was very small ($N = 10$), results should be interpreted with great caution: both parents and children were more likely to show "no response" and were significantly *less* likely to show either Duchenne or non-Duchenne smiles after children failed on the hard puzzle. Parents also showed a reduced probability of looking at their children after children failed on the hard puzzle. Thus, both parents and toddlers were more likely to display non-Duchenne smiles and to look at the other following an improbable or unnecessary failure to meet a standard—failure on an easy task—than following an expectable outcome—success on an easy task or failure on a very difficult task.

Finally, parents often made the hard puzzle easier by partially completing it and the easy puzzle harder by requiring the child to match colors of puzzle pieces to the puzzle (which was not necessary in order to complete the puzzle), and children smiled most on these intermediate-difficulty-level tasks (easy made hard and hard made easy) (Nelson, 1994). It seems quite possible that parents decided to make the tasks harder or easier in part because of their children's responses. This possibility needs to be explored directly in the future. In summary, parents' and children's responses to the children's failure and success were exceedingly similar, which is consistent with the possibility that parents were reacting to children's reactions to at least some extent. Moreover, both parents and children were more responsive to the unexpected failure on an easy puzzle, perhaps because there is more of a need to establish future needs and goals or to make it clear that one knows the standards in such a context. However, again, direct evidence is lacking that children were communicating their needs, goals, desires, and so forth to their parents, or that their parents were conveying their sense of what level of performance was satisfactory.

5. *Children's emotion communication functions to convey to parents (and probably other socializing agents) that children are uncertain about a social rule.* Sometimes emotion communication serves to help the child determine boundaries—whether the socializing agent "really means it," how important the rule is, or whether a particular behavior violates a standard (see Bateson, Jackson, Haley, and Weakland, 1956, regarding metacommunication). Anecdotal information suggests that children often smile and look at a socializing agent to determine such subtleties. In Klinnert's (1981) original dissertation study, which marked the beginnings of the work on social referencing, she found that toddlers (but not younger babies) often smiled in response to the exaggerated "fear face" used to convey that the babies should not approach various remote-controlled toys. In Cummings' early work on "background anger" (Cummings, 1987), he found that children often smiled while observing adults who were arguing. Virtually all of us have observed a toddler reach toward a potted plant or run toward a street and then stop, turn, and smile at an adult who is watching. These smiles seem to communicate that the child is testing limits or boundaries. Is the mother in Klinnert's study really afraid of the remote controlled spider? Are the people in Cummings' study really acting so mean to one another right in front of a child? Do I really need to refrain from pulling over the plant or running into traffic? These seem to be the questions the child is asking with his or her smile. Although we know of no systematic empirical evidence of this process, we believe that it contributes to the socialization of guilt and shame by helping children to verify standards and infractions of standards by seeking information from a socializing agent.

6. *Children's emotion communication tells parents (or other socializing agents) that the children understand and care that they have upheld or violated a social standard.* Shameful (or embarrassed), prideful, and guilty displays do seem quite relevant to social communication that one has violated or adhered to a social rule. In shame or embarrassment, individuals typically avert their gaze from others, shrink away from others' view, and try to avoid contact with them. All of these actions would seem to function as submissive/appeasement gestures that indicate to others that one is "lower" than the observing other. When displayed in the context of failure to meet standards, it makes sense that they communicate deference to the rules or standards that the other is deemed to hold.

Pride responses include sitting tall in an "open posture" (Stipek, Recchia, and McClintic, 1992), smiling, and otherwise showing off one's accomplishment. Guilt is typically associated with confession and making reparation. Both of these sets of responses, even more clearly than shameful responses, indicate the offender's acknowledgment of standards: either success in relation to the standard (pride) or wrongdoing in relation to it. Moreover, there is evidence that children of a variety of ages display these behaviors (or report themselves doing so) when they appear to be involved in these emotions (for example, Alessandri and Lewis, 1993; Barrett, Zahn-Waxler, and Cole, 1993; Ferguson and Stegge, 1995; Lewis, Sullivan, Stanger, and Weiss, 1989; Stipek, Recchia, and McClintic, 1992). What is somewhat less clear empirically is just what these behaviors actually communicate to others during ongoing interactions.

Most researchers and theorists who write about shame and pride agree that these emotions occur when one evaluates one's behavior vis-à-vis some standard, rule, or goal (see, for example, Barrett, 1995; Heckhausen, 1984; Lewis, Sullivan, Stanger, and Weiss, 1989; Stipek, 1995). According to such approaches, the requirement that behavior be *evaluated* in relation to a standard or goal sets pride and shame apart from emotions such as joy or pleasure and sadness or frustration/anger. One cannot simply be excited about a stimulus display or upset that the stimulus display is not available; one must be excited about *one's accomplishment,* or upset about *one's failure.* For this reason, such researchers often interpret displays of pride, shame, or guilt behaviors as indicators that children understand and care that they have adhered to or violated a social rule. Heckhausen (1984), for example, suggested that "a sense of personal competence" does not develop until after three years of age, based on his observation of children's pride- and shame-relevant responses to success or failure on a competitive task (making a tower more quickly than someone else can make one). However, when the goal was obvious and intrinsic to the task, rather than competitive, Stipek, Recchia, and McClintic (1992) found that children showed apparent pride and shame much earlier, which they too interpreted as meaning that evaluation with respect to standards was possible.

Stipek, Recchia, and McClintic (1992) found that even infants as young as thirteen months of age smiled and looked up at the experimenter (E) after they accomplished an unambiguous goal. At all ages, from thirteen to thirty-nine months of age, some toddlers were more likely to look up at E if they accomplished the goal than if E accomplished the goal; however, the difference in amount of looking up at E for their own versus E's accomplishments was significant only for toddlers who were in the twenty-two-month or older groups. In free play, children who were thirteen or fifteen months old were as likely as older toddlers to smile, exclaim, and/or clap after accomplishing something; however, with age more children were likely to call others' attention to their accomplishments (although some children of all age groups did so). Moreover, by twenty-four months of age (the youngest age tested in the follow-up study addressing shame), Stipek, Recchia, and McClintic found that children smiled and had an open posture more often when they succeeded, and avoided eye contact and had a closed posture more often when they failed.

Both Heckhausen and Stipek and colleagues interpreted their findings as indicating that children could evaluate their accomplishments vis-à-vis goals, given that such an ability was deemed prerequisite to these emotions. However, there was no independent evidence that children could do so, and no children under thirteen months were studied, leaving the question of the development of this ability unanswered.

In her own ongoing work, author Barrett has found that children as young as eleven months of age react more positively to success than to failure, even when their parent is not reacting more positively to success than failure (Barrett, MacPhee, and Sullivan, 1992). These were reactions to outcomes rather than to process, which is one criterion that Stipek, Recchia, and McClintic (1992) use to distinguish pride responses from mastery pleasure; however, some still might suggest that these responses did not necessarily involve or communicate "true pride" (see, for example, Stipek, 1995).

Kagan (1981) placed the emergence of children's ability to evaluate their behavior vis-à-vis standards at around the middle of the second year of life, based on observations of toddlers' "anxiety" when they could not follow a model's pretense actions, and on their excessive concern about flawed objects (which Kagan interpreted as stemming from concern about who broke the objects). Thus he inferred such evaluation on the basis of a more general category of negative affect, in the context of standard violations. Again, however, direct evidence was lacking that the children's anxiety communicated their knowledge of standards to those with whom they interacted.

A couple of studies at least have examined the relation between an independent assessment of children's understanding of standards and their shame- and pride-relevant behavior. To our knowledge, only one study has examined toddlers' standard sensitivity in relation to shame- and guilt-relevant behavior (Kochanska, Casey, and Fukumoto, 1995), and one has studied them in relation to pride-relevant behavior (Bullock and Lutkenhaus, 1988). Kochanska, Casey, and Fukumoto's (1995) distress/escape aggregated variable involves primarily shamelike, not guiltlike, responses to two situations in which toddlers appeared to have damaged the experimenter's possessions (high distress/withdrawal, infrequency of commenting about the mishap after harming E's possession, and low reparation). In addition, two other aggregated variables involving toddlers' responses to the same situation seemed guilt-relevant: one, which was labeled "confession/reparative attempts," involved taking responsibility for the wrongdoing and trying physically to repair it; the other, labeled "apology/reparative comments," included apologies and statements about making reparation, and seemed more oriented toward reestablishing a good relationship with the experimenter. All three of these variables were correlated with two- to three-and-a-half-year-old children's verbal and physical concern about flawed objects and their preference for and positive comments about unflawed objects.

Results indicated that boys who made more positive comments about unflawed objects showed more shamelike responses when they thought they had harmed E's possessions. Conversely, girls who showed more verbal and physical concern about flawed objects (for example, talking about or touching the flaws) were more likely to show shamelike behavior when they thought they had harmed E's possessions. In addition, girls who took greater responsibility for, and tried to repair the damage to, E's possessions were more likely to display both physical and verbal concern about the flawed objects, and girls who apologized and made reparative comments made more positive comments about unflawed objects, as well as negative comments about flaws. Boys' guilt-relevant behaviors were not as strongly related to their reactions to the flawed and unflawed objects; only their tendency to apologize and make comments about reparation were associated with a greater degree of verbal concern about flawed objects. Unfortunately, given that the youngest children in this study were twenty-six months of age, this study does not address whether and how sensitivity to standards might be related to shame and/or guilt at younger ages, nor whether standard sensitivity is required for or communicated by shame. Moreover, because pride was not addressed in this study, it provides no information regarding the relation between sensitivity to standard violations and pride. Finally, sensitivity to physical flaws in objects does not clearly indicate sensitivity to behavioral standards.

Bullock and Lutkenhaus's (1988) study of fifteen- to thirty-five-month-olds revealed that although adherence to socially sanctioned standards for achievement increased with age during toddlerhood, only fifteen- to eighteen-month-olds displayed greater attention to standards (as evidenced by having a simple standard, stopping when one meets the standard, taking care to align tower pieces, and making corrections) on tasks on which they displayed pride-relevant responses. It is possible that a ceiling effect on adherence to standards compromised results for older children. However, this study does suggest that even fifteen-month-olds adhere to some simple behavioral standards, and that the extent to which they do is related to their tendency to show pridelike reactions. Again, younger children did not participate in the study, so determination of age of onset of attention to standards or of the effect of such attention on pride behaviors is not available.

It should also be pointed out that Bullock and Lutkenhaus (1988) did not label their affective responses "pride," nor did Kochanska, Casey, and Fukumoto (1995) label their responses "shame"; the responses simply are comparable to those labeled as such in other investigations. Thus many unanswered questions remain.

7. *Parents' (and probably other socializing agents') perception of children's shame, guilt, or pride affects socialization practices even if children's responses would not be construed as shame, guilt, or pride by researchers or theoreticians in the field.* There is some evidence that parents believe that their infants experience emotions such as guilt or pride at ages that are much younger than most theorists and researchers in the field would deem possible (most theorists would say that these emotions are not possible until two, three, or even five years of age). Johnson, Emde, and Pannabecker (1982) asked 597 mothers of babies to indicate whether their child displayed each of ten emotions at the time of the survey, and if so, when their babies had begun to show each emotion. Emotions about which the researchers asked included shyness and guilt. Three mothers said that their babies had displayed guilt as early as one to three months of age, and 49 percent said that their babies had displayed guilt by thirteen to fifteen months of age. Mothers were not asked about pride or shame, but they were asked about shyness, which some theorists consider a variant of shame. Some mothers, again, believed that they had observed shyness in their babies in the first three months of life, and the majority (66 percent) believed that they had observed shyness by seven to nine months of age.

In a different study (Reissland, 1990), mothers were asked if they could elicit pride and happiness in their two- to fifteen-month-old babies. Only two of the seventeen mothers who were asked (a mother of a three-month old and a mother of a six-month old) said that their baby did not yet show pride; all other mothers said they could elicit pride and happiness in their babies, and proceeded to show how they would do so. Mothers of the youngest babies elicited pride by achieving something on the baby's behalf, attributing the achievement to the baby, and praising the baby (for example, the mother of a six-month-old stands the boy up, then praises him). Mothers of older babies expected them to make some effort to achieve something, after which they praised them (for example, a mother requests a twelve-month-old to stand up on his own, and then praises him when he does so successfully). When mothers wished to elicit happiness, in contrast, they typically stimulated the babies in exciting ways (for example, tickling). The fact that parents not only attributed pride to relatively young infants but engaged in characteristic behavior patterns so as to elicit it suggests that parents' own beliefs about their children's emotions play a role in their interactions with and socialization of their children with respect to these emotions. In fact, it seems likely that such interaction patterns help to socially construct these emotions.

Conclusions

In this chapter we have outlined seven postulates regarding the potential impact of emotion communication on the development of pride, shame, and guilt in infancy and toddlerhood. We have presented some evidence that these principles are operative when such evidence is available. Emotions are an important source of communication between socializing agents and both infants and young children. Not only are emotions the object of socialization, they are forces in that socialization process. The development of social emotions helps make infants and young children members of society by making them care about the rules of society. We believe that emotion communication plays crucial roles in this process.

References

Alessandri, S. M., and Lewis, M. "Parental Evaluation and Its Relation to Shame and Pride in Young Children." *Sex Roles,* 1993, *29,* 335–343.

Alessandri, S. M., and Lewis, M. "Differences in Pride and Shame in Maltreated and Non-maltreated Preschoolers." *Child Development,* 1996, *67,* 1857–1869.

Altmann, S. "Primates." In T. Sebeok (ed.), *Animal Communication: Techniques of Study and Results of Research.* Bloomington: Indiana University Press, 1968.

Ausubel, D. P. "Relationship Between Shame and Guilt in the Socialization Process." *Psychological Review,* 1955, *62,* 378–390.

Barrett, K. C. "Origins of Social Emotions and Self-Regulation: Appreciation of 'Right' and 'Wrong.'" In S. Lamb (chair), *The Beginnings of Morality,* symposium presented at the meeting of the Society for Research in Child Development, New Orleans, Mar. 1993a.

Barrett, K. C. "The Development of Nonverbal Communication of Emotion: A Functionalist Perspective." *Journal of Nonverbal Behavior,* 1993b, *17,* 145–169.

Barrett, K. "A Functionalist Approach to Shame and Guilt." In J. P. Tangney and K. W. Fischer (eds.), *Self-Conscious Emotions.* New York: Guilford Press, 1995.

Barrett, K. C. "A Functionalist Approach to the Development of Emotion." In M. F. Mascolo and S. Griffin (eds.), *What Develops in Emotional Development?* New York: Plenum, forthcoming.

Barrett, K. C., and Campos, J. J. "Perspectives on Emotional Development: II. A Functionalist Approach to Emotions." In J. Osofsky (ed.), *Handbook of Infant Development.* (2nd ed.) New York: Wiley, 1987.

Barrett, K. C., MacPhee, D., and Sullivan, S. "Development of Social Emotions and Self-Regulation." Paper presented at meeting of the International Society for Infant Studies, Miami, May 1992.

Barrett, K. C., Zahn-Waxler, C., and Cole, P. M. "Avoiders Versus Amenders—Implications for the Investigation of Guilt and Shame During Toddlerhood?" *Cognition and Emotion,* 1993, *7,* 481–505.

Bateson, G., Jackson, D., Haley, J., and Weakland, J. "Toward a Theory of Schizophrenia." *Behavioral Science,* 1956, *1,* 251–264.

Baumeister, R. F., Stillwell, A. M., and Heatherton, T. F. "Interpersonal Aspects of Guilt: Evidence from Narrative Studies." In J. P. Tangney and K. W. Fischer (eds.), *Self-Conscious Emotions.* New York: Guilford Press, 1995.

Bullock, M., and Lutkenhaus, P. "The Development of Volitional Behavior in the Toddler Years." *Child Development,* 1988, *59,* 664–674.

Chevalier-Skolnikoff, S. "Facial Expression of Emotion in Nonhuman Primates." In P. Ekman (ed.), *Darwin and Facial Expression*. Orlando, Fla.: Academic Press, 1973.

Cummings, E. M. "Coping with Background Anger in Early Childhood." *Child Development,* 1987, *58,* 976–984.

Denham, S. A. "Maternal Affect and Toddlers' Social-Emotional Competence." *American Journal of Orthopsychiatry,* 1989, *59,* 368–376.

Denham, S. A. "Maternal Emotional Responsiveness and Toddlers' Social-Emotional Competence." *Journal of Child Psychology and Psychiatry and Allied Disciplines,* 1993, *34,* 715–728.

Denham, S. A., Renwick, S., and Hewes, S. "Emotional Communication Between Mothers and Preschoolers: Relations with Social-Emotional Competence." *Merrill-Palmer Quarterly,* 1994, *40,* 488–508.

Ekman, P., and Friesen, W. V. "Felt, False, and Miserable Smiles." *Journal of Nonverbal Behavior,* 1982, *6,* 238–252.

Ferguson, T. J., and Stegge, H. "Emotional States and Traits in Children: The Case of Guilt and Shame." In J. P. Tangney and K. W. Fischer (eds.), *Self-Conscious Emotions.* New York: Guilford Press, 1995.

Ferguson, T. J., Stegge, H., and Damhuis, I. "Children's Understanding of Guilt and Shame." *Child Development,* 1991, *62,* 827–839.

Fridlund, A. "Evolution and Facial Action in Reflex, Social Motive, and Paralanguage." *Biological Psychology,* 1991, *32,* 3–100.

Geppert, U. *A Coding-System for Analyzing Behavioral Expressions of Self-Evaluated Emotions (Technical Manual).* Munich: Max Plank Institute for Psychological Research, 1986.

Gianino, A., and Tronick, E. "The Mutual Regulation Model: The Infant's Self and Interactive Regulation and Coping and Defensive Capabilities." In T. Field, P. McCabe, and N. Schneiderman (eds.), *Stress and Coping,* Vol. 2. Hillsdale, N.J.: Erlbaum, 1988.

Heckhausen, H. "Emergent Achievement Behavior: Some Early Developments." In J. Nicholls (ed.), *Advances in Motivation and Achievement,* Vol. 3: *The Development of Achievement Motivation.* Greenwich, Conn.: JAI Press, 1984.

Izard, C. *Human Emotions.* New York: Plenum, 1977.

Izard, C., and Malatesta, C. "Perspectives on Emotional Development I: Differential Emotions Theory of Early Emotional Development." In J. Osofsky (ed.), *Handbook of Infant Development.* New York: Wiley, 1987.

Johnson, W. F., Emde, R. N., and Pannabecker, B. J. "Maternal Perception of Infant Emotion from Birth Through Eighteen Months." *Infant Behavior and Development,* 1982, *5,* 313–322.

Jones, S. S., and Ragg, T. "Smile Production in Older Infants: The Importance of a Social Recipient for the Facial Signal." *Child Development,* 1989, *60,* 811–818.

Kagan, J. *The Second Year: The Emergence of Self-Awareness.* Cambridge, Mass.: Harvard University Press, 1981.

Keltner, D., and Buswell, B. N. "Evidence for the Distinctness of Embarrassment, Shame, and Guilt: A Study of Recalled Antecedents and Facial Expressions of Emotion." *Cognition and Emotion,* 1996, *10,* 155–171.

Kitayama, S., and Markus, H. R. "Introduction to Cultural Psychology and Emotion Research." In S. Kitayama and H. R. Markus (eds.), *Emotion and Culture.* Washington, D.C.: American Psychological Association, 1994.

Kitayama, S., Markus, H. R., and Matsumoto, H. "Culture, Self, and Emotion: A Cultural Perspective on Self-Conscious Emotions." In J. P. Tangney and K. W. Fischer (eds.), *Self-Conscious Emotions.* New York: Guilford Press, 1995.

Klinnert, M. D. "Infants' Use of Mothers' Facial Expressions for Regulating Their Own Behavior." Unpublished doctoral dissertation, University of Denver, 1981.

Klinnert, M., Campos, J., Sorce, J., Emde, R., and Svejda, M. "Emotions as Behavior Regulators: Social Referencing in Infancy." In R. Plutchik and H. Kellerman (eds.), *Emotion: Theory, Research, and Experience,* Vol. 2. Orlando, Fla.: Academic Press, 1983.

Kochanska, G., and Aksan, N. "Mother-Child Mutually Positive Affect, the Quality of Child Compliance to Requests and Prohibitions, and Maternal Control as Correlates of Early Internalization." *Child Development,* 1995, *66,* 236–254.

Kochanska, G., Casey, R. J., and Fukumoto, A. "Toddlers' Sensitivity to Standard Violations." *Child Development,* 1995, *66,* 643–656.

Lewis, H. B. *Shame and Guilt in Neurosis.* New York: International Universities Press, 1971.

Lewis, M. "The Development of Anger and Rage." In S. P. Roose and R. Glick (eds.), *Rage, Power, and Aggression: Their Relationship to Motivation and Aggression.* New Haven, Conn.: Yale University Press, 1990.

Lewis, M., Alessandri, S., and Sullivan, M. "Differences in Shame and Pride as a Function of Children's Gender and Task Difficulty." *Child Development,* 1992, *63,* 630–638.

Lewis, M., Sullivan, M., Stanger, C., and Weiss, M. "Self Development and Self-Conscious Emotions." *Child Development,* 1989, *60,* 146–156.

Lindsay-Hartz, J., de Rivera, J., and Mascolo, M. F. "Differentiating Guilt and Shame and Their Effects on Motivation." In J. P. Tangney and K. W. Fischer (eds.), *Self-Conscious Emotions.* New York: Guilford Press, 1995.

Londerville, S., and Main, M. "Security of Attachment, Compliance, and Maternal Training Methods in the Second Year of Life." *Developmental Psychology,* 1981, *17,* 289–298.

Maccoby, E., and Martin, J. "Socialization in the Context of the Family: Parent-Child Interaction." In P. Mussen (ed.), *Handbook of Child Psychology,* Vol. 4: *Socialization, Personality, and Social Development,* New York: Wiley, 1983.

Malatesta, C., and Haviland, J. "Learning Display Rules: The Socialization of Emotional Expression in Infancy." *Child Development,* 1982, *53,* 991–1003.

Marler, P. "Communication in Monkeys and Apes." In I. DeVore (ed.), *Primate Behavior: Field Studies of Monkeys and Apes.* New York: Henry Holt, 1965.

Mead, G. H. "The Genesis of the Self and Social Control." *International Journal of Ethics,* 1925, *35,* 251–273.

Menon, U., and Shweder, R. A. "Kali's Tongue: Cultural Psychology and the Power of Shame in Orissa, India." In S. Kitayama and H. R. Markus (eds.), *Emotion and Culture.* Washington, D.C.: American Psychological Association, 1994.

Messinger, D. S. "The Development of Infant Smiling: A Dynamic Systems Approach." *Dissertation Abstracts International,* 1994, *55,* 1201.

Miyake, K., and Yamazaki, K. "Self-Conscious Emotions, Child-Rearing, and Child Psychopathology in Japanese Culture." In J. P. Tangney and K. W. Fischer (eds.), *Self-Conscious Emotions.* New York: Guilford Press, 1995.

Nelson, G. C. "The Functional Significance of Types of Smiles During Parent-Child Interactions." Unpublished master's thesis, Colorado State University, 1994.

Nelson, G. C., and Barrett, K. C. "Sequences of Affect Communication Between Parents and Toddlers During Easy and Difficult Tasks." Paper presented at the Society for Research in Child Development meetings, Washington, D.C., Apr. 3, 1997.

Parke, R. D., Cassidy, J., Burks, V. M., Carson, J. L., and Boyum, L. "Familial Contributions to Peer Competence Among Young Children: The Role of Interactive and Affective Processes." In R. D. Parke and G. W. Ladd (eds.), *Family-Peer Relationships: Modes of Linkage.* Hillsdale, N.J.: Erlbaum, 1992.

Parpal, M., and Maccoby, E. E. "Maternal Responsiveness and Subsequent Child Compliance." *Child Development,* 1985, *56,* 1326–1334.

Patterson, G. R., and Cobb, J. A. "A Dyadic Analysis of Aggressive Behaviors." In J. P. Hill (ed.), *Minnesota Symposium on Child Psychology,* Vol. 5. Minneapolis: University of Minnesota Press, 1971.

Reissland, N. "Parental Frameworks of Pleasure and Pride." *Infant Behavior and Development,* 1990, *13,* 249–256.

Reissland, N. "The Socialization of Pride in Young Children." *International Journal of Behavioral Development,* 1994, *17,* 541–552.

Rocissano, L., Slade, A., and Lynch, V. "Dyadic Synchrony and Toddler Compliance." *Developmental Psychology,* 1987, *23,* 698–704.

Scherer, K. R., Walbott, H. G., Matsumoto, D., and Kudoh, T. "Emotional Experience in Cultural Context: A Comparison Between Europe, Japan, and the United States." In K. R. Scherer (ed.), *Facets of Emotion.* Hillsdale, N.J.: Erlbaum, 1988.

Silverman, I. W., and Ragusa, D. M. "Child and Maternal Correlates of Impulse Control in Twenty-Four-Month-Old Children." *Genetic, Social, and General Psychology Monographs,* 1990, *116,* 435–473.

Sroufe, L. A. "Socioemotional Development." In J. Osofsky (ed.), *Handbook of Infant Development.* New York: Wiley, 1979.

Stipek, D. "The Development of Pride and Shame in Toddlers." In J. P. Tangney and K. W. Fischer (eds.), *Self-Conscious Emotions.* New York: Guilford Press, 1995.

Stipek, D. J., Recchia, S., and McClintic, S. "Self-Evaluation in Young Children." *Monographs of the Society for Research in Child Development,* 1992, *57* (1, Serial No. 226).

Tangney, J. P. "Shame and Guilt in Interpersonal Relationships." In J. P. Tangney and K. W. Fischer (eds.), *Self-Conscious Emotions.* New York: Guilford Press, 1995.

Trevarthen, C. "Emotions in Infancy: Regulators of Contact and Relationships with Persons." In K. R. Scherer and P. Ekman (eds.), *Approaches to Emotion.* Hillsdale, N.J.: Erlbaum, 1984.

Walbott, H. G., and Scherer, K. R. "Cultural Determinants in Experiencing Shame and Guilt." In J. P. Tangney and K. W. Fischer (eds.), *Self-Conscious Emotions.* New York: Guilford Press, 1995.

Walden, T. A. "Infant Social Referencing." In J. Garber and K. Dodge (eds.), *The Development of Emotion Regulation and Dysregulation.* New York: Cambridge University Press, 1991.

KAREN CAPLOVITZ BARRETT is associate professor in human development and family studies at Colorado State University.

G. CHRISTINA NELSON-GOENS is a doctoral candidate in the Department of Psychology at the University of Utah.

Both similarities and differences are found across cultures when observers make judgments of infants' emotions.

Observer Judgments of Emotion in American, Japanese, and Chinese Infants

Linda A. Camras, Harriet Oster, Joseph J. Campos, Rosemary Campos, Tatsuo Ujiie, Kazuo Miyake, Wang Lei, Meng Zhaolan

Cross-cultural studies of infant emotional responses can shed light on the origins of group differences in adult emotional behavior as well as on the processes involved in emotional development both within and across cultures. In the United States, a number of laboratory procedures have been developed that are thought to evoke emotions such as fear (for example, stranger approach; see Campos, Emde, Gaensbauer, and Henderson, 1975), surprise (for example, object concept studies; see Bower, 1967), distress (for example, the Strange Situation; see Ainsworth and Bell, 1970), and anger (for example, arm restraint; see Stenberg, Campos, and Emde, 1983). Examining similarities and differences in the responses of American and non-American babies to these procedures may result in a better understanding of emotional development that may guide future efforts to identify the causal antecedents of their emotional responses.

The several authors are involved in a cross-cultural collaborative study of infant emotional expression supported in part by NIMH Grant MH-47543. We extend our appreciation to our student assistants: Craig Bohm, Jesse Harriot, Kin Ching Kong, Sarah Geenan, Beth Holland, and Brit Creelman. Correspondence, reprint requests, and inquiries regarding the institutional affiliations of the authors should be addressed to Linda A. Camras, Department of Psychology, DePaul University, 2219 N. Kenmore St., Chicago, Illinois, 60614 or lcamras@wppost.depaul.edu.

Emotion Measurement

Characterizing cultural differences in emotional responses requires a broad-based approach to affect measurement because even infants manifest their emotions through a variety of facial, vocal, and bodily actions (Barrett and Campos, 1987; Camras, Sullivan, and Michel, 1993; Malatesta, 1981). Furthermore, emotion researchers have not reached a consensus about either facial or nonfacial criteria that may be used to identify infant emotions (Izard and others, 1995; Oster, Hegley, and Nagel, 1992). Therefore, a useful initial approach to studying cross-cultural differences in infant emotion involves obtaining affect judgments from raters who are unconstrained by a predetermined set of coding criteria. Such judgments are not unalloyed emotion measures but rather reflect what is being communicated to the observer. Nonetheless, within the adult emotion literature, such observer judgments have been accorded a respectable place, for example, providing the basis for contemporary theories of emotional facial expressions (Ekman, Sorenson, and Friesen, 1969).

In the present study, we collected observer judgments of infant emotional responses as an initial step in a larger investigation of American, Japanese, and Chinese infants' facial expressions of emotion. These data (in conjunction with subsequent objective coding of the infants' facial behavior) will enable us to address several questions regarding the universality and ontogeny of infant facial expression. For example, we can determine whether American, Japanese, and Chinese infants produce different variants of prototypical emotional facial expressions identified for adults.

Cross-Cultural Studies of Emotion

For adults, both similarities and differences in emotion have been demonstrated across cultures (see Kitayama and Markus, 1994; Mesquita and Frijda, 1992, for reviews). For example, a strong and consistent body of evidence indicates that prototypical emotional facial expressions are identified similarly in both literate and preliterate societies (Ekman, 1994). Yet cultures may differ greatly in their norms for displaying these expressions in public (Ekman, 1973). Furthermore, societies differ in their culturally dictated appraisal of certain events and this leads to different characteristic emotional responses (for example, fear rather than anger in response to frustration; see Robarchek, 1977; see also Mauro, Sato, and Tucker, 1992). Cultural differences in linguistically specified emotion concepts have also been extensively documented (see, for example, Lutz, 1988; Russell, 1991).

Studies of Asian, Asian American, and European American Infants. Although prelinguistic infants may be subject to fewer social and linguistic constraints than adults, cross-cultural differences in their emotional responding undoubtedly occur. Indeed, some past studies have reported differences between Asian and European American infants in positive and/or negative affect as well as general arousability and activity level (for reviews, see Bornstein, 1989; Chen and Miyake, 1986; Miyake, Campos, Bradshaw, and Kagan, 1986). Results, however, have not been completely consistent across cultures, emotions, age, and eliciting contexts.

Freedman (1974) reported that European American neonates were more irritable and difficult to console than their Chinese American counterparts during the Brazelton testing procedure. Similarly, Kagan and others (1994) found that four-month-old American infants cried and fretted more than Chinese babies in Beijing and were also more active and more vocal. In contrast, after the first half year, European American infants showed *less* negative emotion than Chinese American infants in response to separation from mother (Kagan, Kearsley, and Zelazo, 1978). European American infants were also less inhibited in the presence of unfamiliar peers. With respect to positive emotions, differences among cultural groups have not been observed during the first six months (Kagan and others, 1994; Kagan, Kearsley, and Zelazo, 1978). However, Kagan, Kearsley, and Zelazo found that after six months of age European American infants smiled more than Chinese American babies during developmental testing procedures.

Regarding Japanese infants, Freedman (1974) reported that neonates of Japanese ancestry in both Hawaii and Kobe (Japan) were less prone to distress than European American infants (although they were more prone to distress than Chinese American infants). In contrast, Kosawa (1980, cited in Azuma, 1982) found Japanese neonates to be more irritable than European American infants during the Brazelton examination. At older ages, similarly inconsistent results have been reported for both distress reactions (Lewis, 1989; Lewis, Ramsey, and Kawakami, 1993; Camras and others, 1992) and general activity level (Bornstein, 1989).

Asian and European American Mother-Infant Relationships. If European American and Asian infants do indeed differ in their emotional responsiveness, one source of their dissimilarity might be cultural influences on their social and/or nonsocial environments. Japanese mothers are often described as differing from American mothers in ways that could affect their infants' emotional development. For example, Japanese mothers are reported both to assume and to desire a closer infant-mother interdependence than do European American mothers (Caudill and Weinstein, 1969; Chen and Miyake, 1986; Doi, 1973; Lebra, 1976; Miyake, Campos, Bradshaw, and Kagan, 1986). Conversely, European American mothers are more concerned with fostering autonomy and independence than are Japanese mothers. These differences in beliefs and goals are manifested in cultural practices such as infant carrying and co-sleeping, which are more extensive among Japanese mothers than among American mothers. Japanese mothers are also reported to be more indulgent toward their infants than European American mothers, and to be more concerned with minimizing infant crying in the home. During laboratory interactions (Bornstein and others, 1992; Fogel, Toda, and Kawai, 1988), differences in overall maternal responsiveness or facial/vocal expressiveness have not been observed. However, Japanese mothers engage in more contingent nonverbal behavior than European American mothers and less often direct their infants' attention toward the extradyadic environment.

Although fewer researchers and scholars have focused on Chinese mothers' attitudes and behaviors toward young infants, some differences between European American mothers and Chinese mothers have been described. Chinese mothers are reported to be very indulgent and lenient toward infants, who are considered to be not yet capable of "understanding" (Ho, 1986). At the same time, Chinese American mothers are not thought either to value or to encourage the expression of positive emotion as much as European American mothers (Kagan, Kearsley, and Zelazo, 1978). Kagan invoked this latter difference to explain his finding that Chinese American and European American infants did not differ in smiling during the first half year, but European American infants smiled more than the Chinese American infants after the first six months. In addition, Campos (personal communication, March 14, 1996) has noted that Chinese infants in Beijing are constrained in their motor activity more than American infants by both their clothing and their mothers' behavior.

Such differences in both their social and nonsocial experiences might produce important differences in Asian and European American infants' emotional development. For example, the indulgence experienced by Asian infants might result in fewer and/or less intense experiences of negative affect in their daily lives relative to European American infants. At the same time, when Asian infants do encounter a failure of indulgence or adult unresponsiveness, they might react more negatively than European American infants. In addition, differing experiences with respect to the encouragement of independence versus interdependence might cause Asian and European American infants to differ in their appraisal of some specific eliciting circumstances and thus to differ in their emotional reactions. For example, the constraints on Asian infants' motor activity might slow the epigenetic process through which infants develop expectations regarding the efficacy of their motor actions (Campos, Bertenthal, and Kermoian, 1992). Without such expectations, Asian infants might less readily appraise physical restraint as an impediment and respond to it with less distress. In summary, Asian and European American infants might differ in both their overall experience of emotions and in the specific circumstances under which particular emotions will be elicited.

Laboratory Studies of Infant Emotions

The research and theory just described suggest that further systematic studies of American, Japanese, and Chinese infants' emotional responses are called for. Among American infants, anger, fear, and surprise are three emotions that have been widely studied in the laboratory. For example, Campos and his colleagues (Hiatt, Campos, and Emde, 1979; Stenberg, Campos, and Emde, 1983) employed an arm restraint procedure that was predicted for theoretical reasons to be a potential anger elicitor in infants. To study surprise expressions, Hiatt,

Campos and Emde utilized an object-concept-violation procedure, similar to those assumed to evoke this emotion in cognitive developmental studies (for example, Bower, 1967). Numerous studies have investigated stranger approach as a fear or wariness elicitor in infants (for example, Campos, Emde, Gaensbauer, and Henderson, 1975). In addition Campos and his colleagues (Campos and others, 1978) have used the visual cliff to evoke mild fear. In all these cases, procedures were developed based on widely held beliefs about the elicitors of emotion in infants. In addition, the investigators observed infants' nonfacial responses to these procedures that were interpreted as being consistent with the intended emotion.

The Present Study

Overview. In the present study, we investigated American, Japanese, and Chinese infants' responses to laboratory procedures designed to evoke the emotions of anger/frustration, fear, and surprise. For anger/frustration and surprise we employed two procedures (arm restraint and vanishing object) used in previous studies of American infants. For fear, we developed a novel procedure (presentation of a growling toy gorilla head) that we hoped would evoke a more intense emotional response than has been typically found in previous studies. To measure infants' emotional responses, we asked judges to rate each infant's emotional response after viewing edited videotapes of our procedures on which the babies' facial expression cues were eliminated. We chose to eliminate facial cues to permit us to determine subsequently whether the infant's facial configurations (viewed on separate tapes) suggested the same emotion that observers had judged to be present based on nonfacial cues. In our first step toward this goal, we employed only American raters. Although we expected emotion ratings to differ among American, Chinese, and Japanese raters, our procedure nonetheless enabled us to determine whether infants differed across situation and culture when they were all judged by the same set of raters.

To evaluate our data, we employed a strategy suggested in Hiatt, Campos, and Emde's (1979) earlier study of emotional facial expressions. That is, for each procedure, we determined whether the predicted emotion was given higher ratings than emotions that were predicted for the other procedures. For example, in the growling gorilla situation, were the fear ratings higher than the surprise, anger, and frustration ratings? In addition, we compared across situations to determine whether emotions predicted for a given paradigm were rated higher in that situation than in other situations. For example, were the fear ratings higher in the growling gorilla situation than in the arm restraint and vanishing object procedures? These analyses correspond to Hiatt, Campos, and Emde's (1979) analyses of *intratask specificity* and *intertask specificity* respectively.

Raters. The raters were sixty male and sixty female undergraduate students who participated in partial fulfillment of an introductory psychology course requirement. Raters' ethnic backgrounds were approximately 85 percent European American, 9 percent African American, 4 percent Latino American, and 2 percent Asian American.

Videotape Stimuli. Twelve edited videotapes (four per culture) were prepared from master tapes of infants and their mothers participating in the three emotion-eliciting procedures. Each edited tape contained fifteen to twenty-one episodes, with each episode showing a baby participating in either the arm restraint, vanishing object, or growling gorilla procedure. With two exceptions, each tape showed an equal number of episodes from the three procedures. (Only two of the three procedures were recorded for one Japanese infant and one Chinese infant). Within each culture, babies and procedural episodes were randomly assigned to one of four tapes and randomly ordered on the tape.

The camera was positioned to capture the infant's full body. However, occasionally the infant's leg movements were obscured by the experimenter or because the field of the camera's zoom lens was positioned too close to the infant. On the edited tapes the baby's face was replaced by a small black circle that tracked the baby's head movements. The videotapes also showed the mother sitting beside the infant and the experimenter administering the arm restraint procedure.

The infants shown on the videotapes were eleven-month-old babies from Berkeley, California; Fukushima, Japan; and Beijing, People's Republic of China. There were twenty-four American, twenty-four Japanese, and twenty-one Chinese infants (half males and half females). Each baby participated in all three procedures. Presentation order was balanced across sex and culture. During the procedures, the infants were seated in a high chair while their mothers sat in a chair on their right side, facing perpendicular to the baby. Mothers were instructed to remain passive during the emotion-eliciting procedures.

In the arm restraint procedure, a female experimenter gently grasped the infant's wrists and held them immobile on the table tray for up to three minutes. Experimenters were instructed to release the infant before the time limit if the infant showed seven seconds of continuous crying. Most infants were terminated before the three-minute maximum ($n = 20$ American infants, $n = 22$ Japanese infants, $n = 16$ Chinese infants). There were no significant differences among cultures in the duration of the restraint episodes ($t = 88.5$ sec, 76 sec, and 92 sec for the American, Japanese, and Chinese babies respectively).

In the vanishing toy procedure, a small barking toy dog that the infant was watching appeared to vanish instantaneously. This illusion was achieved utilizing a very large two-field tachistoscope, each wing measuring 73 centimeters. In the center of the apparatus was a 45 x 60 centimeter one-way mirror. The mechanical toy dog was placed behind the mirror approximately 1.58 meters in front of the infant. When light intensity was changed from one wing to another, the object appeared to vanish. At the start of the procedure, the barking toy dog was presented visibly to the infant for fifteen seconds or until the infant looked at the dog. The dog then appeared to disappear for fifteen seconds while the barking could still be heard. This sequence was repeated once.

The fear eliciting procedure involved a disembodied toy gorilla head that could be remotely activated to emit loud unpleasant growling noises while its eyes lit up and its lips moved. To start the procedure, the experimenter (who was hidden behind a curtain) placed the gorilla head on a table approximately 120 centimeters from the infant. After ten seconds, the gorilla was remotely activated to emit six growls. After the growls, the experimenter moved the silent gorilla head fifteen centimeters closer to the infant. This sequence was repeated up to three times. Again, the experimenter was instructed to terminate the procedure early if the infant showed seven seconds of continuous crying. Although most infants were terminated before completion of the full procedure (n = 17 American infants, n = 17 Japanese infants, n = 11 Chinese infants), there were no significant differences among cultures in the duration of the procedures (t = 85 sec, 85.5 sec, and 95 sec for the American, Japanese, and Chinese infants respectively).

Rating Forms. The rating forms contained three sections. In section one, the rater selected the strongest emotion shown by the baby during the episode from the following list of emotions: happiness, surprise, interest, anger, fear, sadness, disgust, distress, frustration, unspecifiable negative affect, other. The term *frustration* was included in addition to *anger* because in our pilot studies many raters had spontaneously used this label to describe infants' response to the arm restraint procedure. Follow-up inquiries indicated that many undergraduates believe that infants are too cognitively immature to experience anger but can experience frustration, considered by several theorists to be another member of the anger emotion family (Barrett and Campos, 1987).

In section two, the rater was asked to judge "how much you think the baby is experiencing each emotion." For each of the emotions just listed, a seven-point Likert scale was provided. In section three, the rater selected the baby's predominant negative emotion from a list of only the negative emotions. Only the data from Section two (ratings) will be reported here.

Procedure. Each rater viewed (and heard) only one videotape, thus rating babies from one of the three cultures on all three of the emotion-eliciting procedures. Most raters viewed the videotape in small groups, but some viewed it individually. As they viewed the first episode from each procedure, raters were given a brief verbal description of the experimental manipulation.

Results

To compare emotion ratings across procedures for each culture, the data were analyzed in a 3 (culture) x 3 (emotion procedure) MANOVA using each subject's mean ratings for happiness, surprise, interest, anger, frustration, distress, and fear as the dependent variables. The ratings for all other emotions were virtually zero and thus were not included in the analysis.

The analysis yielded a significant main effect for procedure with significant univariate tests for all seven emotions, $F(2, 228)$ = 60.72, 41.15, 140.05, 161.35, 98.47, 514.91, 201.87 for happiness, surprise, anger, fear, distress, frustration, and interest respectively, $p < .001$ for each. Post hoc Tukey tests ($p = .05$) showed that each procedure generated significantly higher ratings for its own predicted emotion than did the other two procedures (see Table 5.1). In addition, happiness and interest were rated highest in the vanishing object procedure while distress was rated highest in the arm restraint procedure.

The MANOVA also yielded a significant main effect for culture with a significant univariate effect for happiness, $F(2, 114) = 4.62$, $p < .02$. There was also a significant culture x procedure interaction with significant univariate tests for happiness, $F(4,228) = 9.78$, $p < .001$, distress, $F(4, 228) = 2.99$, $p < .02$, and surprise, $F(4, 228) = 2.50$, $p < .05$.

Post hoc Tukey tests ($p = .05$) on the happiness ratings showed that the three cultures differed significantly only in the vanishing object procedure (see Figure 5.1.) Here the American babies were rated highest, followed by the Japanese, and then the Chinese babies. Post hoc tests on the distress ratings showed that the three cultures differed significantly only in the arm restraint procedure, with the American babies being rated significantly higher than the Chinese babies ($p = .05$) and near-significantly higher than the Japanese babies (see Figure 5.2). Post hoc tests on the surprise ratings showed that differences between cultures approached significance only for the vanishing object procedure, with the American babies being rated higher than the Japanese or Chinese babies. However, comparing across paradigms within each culture, tests also showed that for the Chinese and Japanese babies, surprise was not rated significantly higher in the vanishing object procedure than in the growling gorilla procedure (see Figure 5.3).

To summarize, results showed that the arm restraint and growling gorilla procedures generated significantly higher ratings for their predicted emotions than did the other procedures. However, for the vanishing object procedure, similar results were obtained only for the American babies. For the Japanese and Chinese infants, surprise ratings were not significantly higher in the vanishing object procedure than in the growling gorilla procedure.

To compare emotion ratings within each paradigm, the ratings for the arm restraint, vanishing object, and growling gorilla procedures were analyzed

Table 5.1. Mean Emotion Ratings for Each Procedure

	Procedure		
Emotion	Arm Restraint	Vanishing Object	Growling Gorilla
Frustration	3.68[a]	.47[b]	.66[b]
Anger	1.79[a]	.13[b]	.17[b]
Surprise	.12[c]	1.10[a]	.74[b]
Fear	.87[b]	.34[c]	2.81[a]
Happiness	.09[c]	1.03[a]	.38[b]
Interest	.14[c]	2.95[a]	2.05[b]
Distress	2.41[a]	.43[c]	1.52[b]

Note: Means in the same row that do not share superscripts differ significantly (Tukey test, $p < .05$).

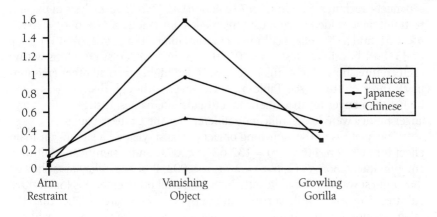

Figure 5.1. Happiness Ratings: Procedure × Culture Interaction

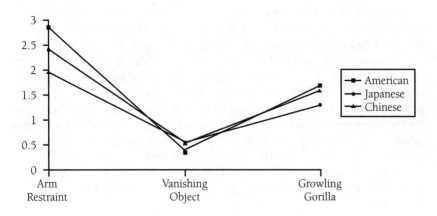

Figure 5.2. Distress Ratings: Procedure × Culture Interaction

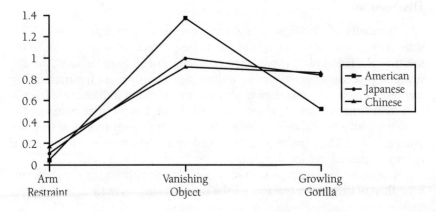

Figure 5.3. Surprise Ratings: Procedure × Culture Interaction

separately, each in a 3 (culture) x 7 (emotion) ANOVA. The analysis of the arm restraint data yielded a significant main effect for emotion, $F(6, 696) = 204.2$, $p < .001$, and a significant culture x emotion interaction, $F(12, 696) = 1.93$, $p < .03$. Post hoc Tukey tests ($p = .05$) that compared across emotions within each culture showed that frustration was rated higher than all other emotions in all three cultures (see Table 5.2). However, although distress was rated higher than anger for the American and Japanese babies, distress ratings and anger ratings were not significantly different for the Chinese babies.

The analysis of the vanishing object data also yielded a significant main effect for emotion, $F(6, 696) = 132.68$, $p < .001$, and a significant culture x emotion interaction, $F(12, 696) = 2.71$, $p < .002$. Post hoc Tukey tests showed that interest was rated significantly higher than all other emotions for all three cultures. However, while surprise and happiness were rated higher than the other emotions for the American and Japanese babies, they were not rated significantly higher than frustration or distress for the Japanese babies, nor frustration, distress, and fear for the Chinese babies.

The analysis of the data from the growling gorilla procedure yielded a significant main effect for emotion, $F(6, 696) = 110.93$, $p < .001$, but no significant effects involving culture. Post hoc Tukey ($p = .05$) analyses showed that fear was rated significantly higher than the other emotions.

To summarize, for all three cultures the growling gorilla procedure generated significantly higher ratings for fear (its predicted emotion) than for the other emotions. Similarly, for all three cultures, the arm restraint procedure generated significantly higher ratings for frustration (a predicted emotion) than for the other emotions. However, the predicted emotion of anger was rated equal or less than distress. In the vanishing object condition, the predicted emotion of surprise was rated higher than the predicted emotions for other procedures (fear, frustration, anger) for the American babies. However, surprise was not significantly higher than several other negative emotions for the Asian babies.

Discussion

Summary of Findings. In the present study, no significant cross-cultural differences were found for two of our three procedures with respect to the selective elicitation of their predicted emotions. For all three cultures, the arm restraint procedure was judged to induce significantly more frustration than any other emotion. Arm restraint also was perceived to induce more frustration than either vanishing object or gorilla head. For all three cultures, the growling gorilla procedure was judged to elicit significantly more fear than any other emotion. The growling gorilla procedure also elicited more fear than the other two procedures for all cultures.

The vanishing object procedure elicited significantly higher ratings of surprise than of frustration and fear for the American babies but was less effective

Table 5.2. Mean Emotion Ratings by Culture and Procedure

	Culture			
Emotion	American	Japanese	Chinese	All
	Arm Restraint			
Frustration	3.91[a]	3.83[a]	3.31[a]	3.68
Distress	2.85[b]	2.40[b]	1.98[b]	2.41
Anger	1.83[c]	1.59[c]	1.93[b]	1.79
Fear	.78[d]	.86[d]	.97[c]	.87
Surprise	.06[e]	.11[e]	.18[d]	.12
Interest	.05[e]	.13[e]	.24[d]	.14
Happiness	.04[e]	.13[e]	.09[c]	.09
	Vanishing Object			
Interest	3.08[a]	3.09[a]	2.68[a]	2.95
Surprise	1.38[b]	.99[b]	.94[b]	1.10
Happiness	1.56[b]	.96[b]	.56[bc]	1.03
Frustration	.45[c]	.55[bc]	.42[be]	.47
Distress	.32[c]	.50[bc]	.48[bc]	.43
Fear	.26[c]	.22[c]	.53[bc]	.34
Anger	.10[c]	.21[c]	.09[c]	.13
	Growling Gorilla			
Fear	3.04	2.76	2.61	2.81[a]
Interest	2.00	2.04	2.12	2.05[b]
Distress	1.66	1.30	1.60	1.52[b]
Surprise	.53	.83	.85	.74[c]
Frustration	.72	.59	.68	.66[c]
Happiness	.27	.50	.39	.38[c]
Anger	.24	.18	.09	.17[c]

Note: Means in the same column that do not share superscripts differ significantly (Tukey test, $p < .05$).

in eliciting such selective judgments for the Japanese and Chinese infants. Like the American babies, the Asian infants were rated higher for surprise than for the emotions of frustration, anger, and fear. However, the differences were of lesser magnitude and often not significant (see Table 5.2). Inspection of the mean ratings showed that the Asian infants were rated both lower on surprise and slightly higher on one or more negative emotions than were the American infants.

Responses to the Vanishing Object. Informal review of the videotapes suggested several modes of behavioral reaction that might have produced this pattern of ratings. During the vanishing object procedure, American babies often leaned forward and remained oriented to the stimulus throughout the procedure. In contrast, some Asian babies turned away from the stimulus after its initial disappearance. In addition, some Asian babies produced negative reactions that were ambiguous with respect to whether they were responses to expectancy violation or to the disappearance of a desirable object (for example, whimpering and looking around the room). Other Asian babies produced responses that may have been interpreted as indicating greater fear than surprise (for example, whimpering and reaching toward the mother). Currently we are conducting a systematic objective coding of the infants' behavioral reactions in order to evaluate these (and other) possibilities. However, our rating data alone are sufficient to indicate that the vanishing object procedure did not produce equivalent ratings across cultures.

Several ecological factors may have contributed to the (nonsignificant) tendency for Asian babies to respond to the vanishing object procedure with less surprise and more negative affect than the American babies. For example, Asian babies were probably less familiar than American babies with toys similar to the barking dog stimulus. This would be consistent with Japanese and Chinese mothers' greater focus on intradyadic interactions and lesser focus on the extradyadic environment. In consequence, Asian babies may have been warier and/or more aroused when first presented with the visible barking toy dog due to their unfamiliarity with such toys. Either of these initial responses might predispose Asian babies to react more negatively to the subsequent expectancy violation (that is, the dog's visual disappearance accompanied by sustained barking). Sroufe, Waters, and Matas (1974) have reported similar effects of unfamiliarity on American infants' reactions to expectancy violation.

Differences Between Chinese and Japanese Infants. Other interesting cross-cultural differences were found for emotions not specifically targeted by our procedures. In the vanishing object procedure, American infants were judged to be significantly happier than the Japanese infants, who were themselves rated significantly happier than the Chinese infants. A similar trend was found for the ratings of distress in the arm restraint condition. These findings suggest that Chinese and Japanese babies differ from each other in emotionality as well as from American babies. However, of equal importance, the cross-cultural differences we observed were selective with respect to emotion and eliciting situation. The babies from all three cultures were judged to respond comparably in many cases.

Frustration and Anger. Our results also showed that American undergraduate raters generally judged the eliciting procedures to produce the emotions predicted by ourselves and previous researchers (Hiatt, Campos, and Emde, 1979; Stenberg, Campos, and Emde, 1983). Partial disagreement was found only for the arm restraint procedure. In previous investigations, arm restraint has been described as an elicitor of anger. However, our judges rated the infants significantly lower on anger than on frustration. As we learned during exit interviews in our pilot studies, naive undergraduates consider frustration to be a more appropriate descriptor of the infants' emotional responses than anger, primarily because of the infants' cognitive immaturity. Thus observers' beliefs about emotion and development as well as the infants' actual behavior influenced raters' judgments of the babies' emotional reactions. Interestingly, in accordance with our raters, one prominent emotion theorist (Lazarus, 1994) has also proposed that infants do not have the cognitive prerequisites for experiencing anger. Nevertheless, according to some perspectives, frustration may also be considered a member of the anger family (Barrett and Campos, 1987). Thus, of primary importance, undergraduates and researchers do agree on the emotion family elicited by arm restraint. Additionally, our results illustrate how the concept of emotion families enables us to explain systematic variability in emotion terminology that might be difficult to accommodate within a theory that focuses too narrowly on single emotion terms.

More generally, our findings with respect to the anger and frustration ratings also suggest that emotion judgments reflect the integration of information from a variety of sources including both the emoter's behavior and the observer's a priori beliefs or knowledge about the emoter and/or the eliciting context. Support for this view can also be found in several previous judgment studies involving older subjects (for example, Gnepp and Gould, 1985). For example, Camras, Sachs-Alter, and Ribordy (1996) showed that children's emotion judgments depend on both the emoter's facial expressions and the judge's knowledge of the emoter's prior experience relevant to the eliciting situation (for example, having been previously bitten by a dog). The importance of confluent information also figures prominently in discussions of expressive "display rules" (for example, social conventions regarding emotional expression; see Ekman, 1972). For example, an observer's knowledge of display rules (for example, how to greet a colleague) will determine how she interprets the smile of a professional rival encountered at a conference meeting.

Future Directions

Asian Raters. As indicated earlier, one limitation of this study was our sole use of American raters rather than judges from all three cultures. Inclusion of non-American raters in future studies will be important in clarifying the interpretation of some of the cultural differences we obtained. For example, Asian babies may have received lower happiness and surprise ratings in the vanishing object procedure than American infants did because our American raters failed to discern the behavioral manifestations of these emotions in the Japanese and Chinese babies. If so, Asian judges might produce a different pattern of emotion ratings than did the American judges (for example, equivalent ratings of surprise and happiness for all three cultures or even higher ratings for the Asian babies). Such findings would suggest a set of further studies to identify the behaviors used by raters in the several cultures as the basis for their differing emotion judgments. While future research may profitably pursue this line of inquiry, the present study's findings suggest that such cross-cultural differences will not be widespread. In our study, few significant cross-cultural differences were found in the emotion ratings for our three procedures.

A second issue that can be addressed through the inclusion of Asian raters is that of cross-cultural differences in emotion concepts. Just as our American raters proposed "frustration" to be more appropriate than "anger" as a descriptor of infants' responses to arm restraint, so might Asian judges characterize infants' responses using emotion concepts that differ from those represented by the English-language terms we used. Several emotion concepts have been identified for Asian cultures that have no exact American equivalents (for example, *amae* for the Japanese; see Doi, 1973). Nonetheless, approximate translations of English-language emotion terms have been successfully employed in studies with Chinese and Japanese subjects (Markham and Lei, 1994; Matsumoto and Ekman, 1989). Thus we have no immediate reason to believe that our emotion terms (or rather approximate translations thereof) would be considered confusing or inappropriate to Asian judges. Nevertheless, exploring possible differences in Asian versus American spontaneous labeling of infants' behavior will make an important contribution to our understanding of emotion concepts in American, Chinese, and Japanese culture.

Facial Expression Analyses. An important goal of our study was to provide data that will inform subsequent investigations of the infants' objectively coded facial expressions. That is, we will examine relationships between the infants' facial behavior and their emotion ratings based only on nonfacial cues. In doing so, we can determine whether infants from our three cultures produce similar or different facial expressions when they are rated similarly on the basis of nonfacial emotion cues. In addition, we can determine whether infants' negative facial expressions differ systematically across situations judged to evoke two different negative emotions. Last, we can conduct empirically driven analyses that may result in our identifying procedure-specific facial patterns not previously described as emotional expressions. If these facial patterns also were found in future studies employing larger sample sizes and different procedures for eliciting the same emotions, we might propose them to be infant-specific affective displays. Through such a research program we will thus be able to address the issue of expressive universality (Ekman, 1994) as well as the current debate regarding the differentiation of infants' negative emotional facial expressions (see Camras, 1991; Izard and others, 1995; Oster, Hegley, and Nagel, 1992).

Conclusion

The present study made several important contributions to our understanding of emotional responding in American, Japanese, and Chinese infants. First, both cross-cultural similarities and differences were found in American observers' ratings of the infants' emotions. Second, the investigation demonstrated that facial cues are not necessary for observers to make systematic judgments of infant emotions. Last, our study served as a necessary first step in the cross-cultural investigation of infant facial expression, allowing us to examine subsequently the coordination between facial patterning and nonfacial measures of emotional reaction. Thus, irrespective of any cultural differences in the emotions evoked by our eliciting procedures, we may yet find evidence for universality in the organization and patterning of infants' facial and nonfacial emotional responses.

References

Ainsworth, M., and Bell, S. "Attachment, Exploration and Separation: Illustrated by the Behavior of One-Year-Olds in a Strange Situation." *Child Development,* 1970, *41* (1), 49–67.

Azuma, H. "Current Trends in Studies of Behavioral Development in Japan." *International Journal of Behavioral Development,* 1982, *5,* 153–169.

Barrett, K. C., and Campos, J. "Perspectives on Emotional Development II: A Functionalist Approach to Emotions." In J. Osofsky (ed.), *Handbook of Infant Development.* (2nd ed.) New York: Wiley, 1987.

Bornstein, M. "Cross-Cultural Developmental Comparisons: The Case of Japanese-American Infant and Mother Activities and Interactions." *Developmental Review,* 1989, *9,* 171–204.

Bornstein, M., Tamis-LeMonda, C., Tal, J., Ludemann, P., Toda, S., Rahn, M., Azuma, H., and Vardi, D. "Maternal Responsiveness to Infants in Three Societies: The United States, France and Japan." *Child Development,* 1992, *63,* 808–821.

Bower, T. "The Development of Object Permanence: Some Studies of Existence Constancy." *Perception and Psychophysics,* 1967, *2* (9), 411–418.

Campos, J., Bertenthal, B., and Kermoian, R. "Early Experience and Emotional Development: The Emergence of Wariness of Heights." *Psychology Science,* 1992, *3,* 61–64.

Campos, J., Emde, R., Gaensbauer, T., and Henderson, C. "Cardiac and Behavioral Inter-Relationships in the Reaction of Infants to Strangers." *Developmental Psychology,* 1975, *11,* 589–601.

Campos, J., Hiatt, S., Ramsay, D., Henderson, C., and Svejda, M. "The Emergence of Fear on the Visual Cliff." In M. Lewis and L. Rosenblum (eds.), *The Development of Affect.* New York: Plenum, 1978.

Camras, L. "Conceptualizing Early Infant Affect: View II and Reply." In K. Strongman (ed.), *International Review of Studies on Emotion.* New York: Wiley, 1991.

Camras, L., Oster, H. O., Campos, J., Miyake, K., and Bradshaw, D. "Japanese and American Infants' Responses to Arm Restraint." *Developmental Psychology,* 1992, *28* (4) 578–583.

Camras, L., Sachs-Alter, E., and Ribordy, S. "Emotion Understanding in Maltreated Children: Recognition of Facial Expressions and Integration with Other Emotion Cues." In M. Lewis and M. Sullivan (eds.), *Emotional Development in Atypical Children.* Hillsdale, N.J.: Erlbaum, 1996.

Camras, L., Sullivan, J., and Michel, G. "Do Infants Express Discrete Emotions? Adult Judgments of Facial, Vocal and Body Actions." *Journal of Nonverbal Behavior,* 1993, *17* (3), 171–186.

Caudill, W., and Weinstein, H. "Maternal Care and Infant Behavior in Japan and America." *Psychiatry,* 1969, *32,* 12–43.

Chen, S., and Miyake, K. "Japanese Studies of Child Development." In H. Stevenson, H. Azuma, and K. Hakuta (eds.), *Child Development and Education in Japan.* New York: Freeman, 1986.

Doi, T. *The Anatomy of Dependence.* Tokyo: Kodansha International, 1973.

Ekman, P. "Universals and Cultural Differences in Facial Expressions of Emotion." In J. Cole (ed.), *Nebraska Symposium on Motivation.* Lincoln: University of Nebraska Press, 1972.

Ekman, P. "Cross-Cultural Studies of Facial Expression." In P. Ekman (ed.), *Darwin and Facial Expression.* Orlando, Fla.: Academic Press, 1973.

Ekman, P. "Strong Evidence for Universals in Facial Expressions: A Reply to Russell's Mistaken Critique." *Psychological Bulletin*, 1994, *115*, 268–287.

Ekman, P., Sorenson, E., and Friesen, W. "Pan-Cultural Elements in Facial Displays of Emotion." *Science*, 1969, *164*, 86–88.

Fogel, A., Toda, S., and Kawai, M. "Mother-Infant Face-to-Face Interaction in Japan and the United States: A Laboratory Comparison Using Three-Month-Old Infants." *Developmental Psychology*, 1988, *24* (3), 398–406.

Freedman, D. G. *Human Infancy: An Evolutionary Perspective.* New York: Halsted Press, 1974.

Gnepp, J., and Gould, M. "The Development of Personalized Inferences: Understanding Other People's Emotional Reactions in Light of Their Prior Experiences." *Child Development*, 1985, *56*, 1455–1464.

Hiatt, S., Campos, J., and Emde, R. "Facial Patterning and Infant Emotional Expression: Happiness, Surprise, and Fear." *Child Development*, 1979, *50*, 1020–1035.

Ho, D. "Chinese Patterns of Socialization." In M. Bond (ed.), *The Psychology of the Chinese People.* New York: Oxford University Press, 1986.

Izard, C., Fantauzzo, C., Castle, J., Haynes, M., Rayias, M., and Putnam, P. "The Ontogeny and Significance of Infants' Facial Expressions in the First Nine Months of Life." *Developmental Psychology*, 1995, *31* (6), 997–1015.

Kagan, J., Arcus, D., Snidman, N., Feng, W., Hendler, J., and Greene, S. "Reactivity in Infants: A Cross-National Comparison." *Developmental Psychology*, 1994, *30* (3), 342–345.

Kagan, J., Kearsley, R., and Zelazo, P. *Infancy: Its Place in Human Development.* Cambridge, Mass.: Harvard University Press, 1978.

Kitayama, S., and Markus, H. R. *Emotion and Culture.* Washington, D.C.: American Psychological Association, 1994.

Lazarus, R. "Meaning and Emotional Development." In P. Ekman and R. Davidson (eds.), *The Nature of Emotion.* New York: Oxford University Press, 1994.

Lebra, T. *Japanese Patterns of Behavior.* Honolulu: The University Press of Hawaii, 1976.

Lewis, M. "Culture and Biology: The Role of Temperament." In P. Zelazo and R. Barr (eds.), *Challenges to Developmental Paradigms.* Hillsdale, N.J.: Erlbaum, 1989.

Lewis, M., Ramsey, D., and Kawakami, K. "Differences Between Japanese Infants and Caucasian American Infants in Behavioral and Cortisol Response to Inoculation." *Child Development*, 1993, *64*, 1722–1731.

Lutz, C. "Ethnographic Perspectives on the Emotion Lexicon." In V. Hamilton, G. Bower, and N. Frijda (eds.), *Cognitive Perspectives on Emotion and Motivation.* Norwell, Mass.: Kluwer, 1988.

Malatesta, C. "Infant Emotion and the Vocal Affect Lexicon." *Motivation and Emotion*, 1981, *5* (1), 1–23.

Markham, R., and Lei, W. *Recognition of Emotion by Chinese and Australian Children.* Unpublished manuscript, 1994.

Matsumoto, D., and Ekman, P. "American-Japanese Cultural Differences in Intensity Ratings of Facial Expressions of Emotion." *Motivation and Emotion*, 1989, *13* (2), 143–157.

Mauro, R., Sato, K., and Tucker, J. "The Role of Appraisal in Human Emotions: A Cross-Cultural Study." *Journal of Personality and Social Psychology*, 1992, *62* (2), 301–317.

Mesquita, B., and Frijda, N. "Cultural Variations in Emotions: A Review." *Psychological Bulletin*, 1992, *112* (2), 179–204.

Miyake, K., Campos, J., Bradshaw, D., and Kagan, J. "Issues in Socioemotional Development." In H. Stevenson, H. Azuma, and K. Hakuta (eds.), *Child Development and Education in Japan.* New York: Freeman, 1986.

Oster, H., Hegley, D., and Nagel, L. "Adult Judgments and Fine-Grained Analysis of Infant Facial Expressions." *Developmental Psychology*, 1992, *28* (6), 1115–1131.

Robarchek, C. "Frustration, Aggression and the Non-Violent Semai." *American Ethnologist,* 1977, *4,* 762–779.

Russell, J. "Culture and the Categorization of Emotion." *Psychological Bulletin,* 1991, *110,* 426–450.

Sroufe, L. A., Waters, E., and Matas, L. "Contextual Determinants of Infant Affective Response." In M. Lewis and L. Rosenblum (eds.), *The Origins of Fear.* New York: Wiley, 1974.

Stenberg, C., Campos, J., and Emde, R. "The Facial Expression of Anger in Seven-Month-Old Infants." *Child Development,* 1983, *54,* 178–184.

LINDA A. CAMRAS is professor of psychology at DePaul University.

HARRIET OSTER is assistant research professor at New York University.

JOSEPH J. CAMPOS is professor of psychology at the University of California, Berkeley.

ROSEMARY CAMPOS is assistant research psychologist at the Institute for Human Development, University of California, Berkeley.

TATSUO UJIIE is professor at the Research and Educational Center for Life-Long Learning, Fukushima University.

KAZUO MIYAKE is professor of clinical psychology at the Health Sciences University of Hokkaido, Japan.

WANG LEI is professor and chair of the Department of Psychology at Beijing University.

MENG ZHAOLAN is professor at Beijing University

Name Index

Abramovitch, R., 63
Ainsworth, M., 89
Aksan, N., 77
Alessandri, S., 75, 78, 81
Altmann, S.,
Anderson, C., 32
Ausubel, D. P., 71
Averill, J. R., 10
Azuma, H., 91

Ballard, M. E., 29, 30, 31, 37
Bargar, J., 32
Barling, J., 33, 37
Barrett, K. C., 6, 7, 8, 9, 10, 12, 34, 45, 69, 70, 71, 72, 73, 74, 75, 79, 81, 82, 90, 95, 101
Bateson, G., 11
Baumeister, R. F., 70, 71
Beardsall, L., 63
Beidler, R. J., 26
Bell, S., 89
Bennett, L. A., 25
Bertenthal, B., 92
Billings, A. G., 32
Bingham, A., 32
Bitman, I., 32
Black, C., 25, 27, 28, 31, 32
Blakeman, B., 31, 32
Bloom, L., 20
Bornstein, M., 91
Bower, G. H., 45
Bower, T., 89, 93
Bowlby, J., 50
Boyum, L. A., 63
Braafladt, N., 28
Bradley, L. G., 28
Bradshaw, D., 91
Braungart, J. M., 53, 63
Brazelton, T. B., 58
Brennan, K. A., 28
Brent, E. E., 25, 27, 31, 32, 33
Bretherton, I., 50
Briggs, J. L., 58
Britt, R., 37
Bronstein, P., 63
Brown, J., 63
Bucky, S. F., 27, 32
Bugethal, D. B., 64

Bullock, M., 82, 83, 84
Burk, J. P., 25
Burrowes, B. D., 58
Buswell, B. N., 79
Butkovsky, L., 53, 63
Buwick, A., 33

Callan, V. J., 33
Campos, J., 6, 7, 10, 12, 34, 45, 69, 70, 71, 72, 74, 89, 90, 91, 92, 93, 95, 100, 101
Campos, R. G., 6, 34
Camras, L., 5, 8, 63, 90, 91, 101, 102
Carroll, A., 32, 33, 38
Casey, R. J., 82, 84
Cassidy, J., 53, 63, 64n
Cate, C. A., 37
Caudill, W., 91
Caulkins, S., 34, 35
Chen, S., 91
Chevalier-Skolnikoff, S., 71
Christopher, F. S., 37
Cicchetti, D., 29, 31, 33, 35, 45, 60, 64n
Clair, D., 25, 28
Cobb, J. A., 77
Cole, P. M., 73, 81
Cooper, M. L., 26
Cork, R. M., 33
Corrigan, P. W., 28
Costanzo, P. R., 46, 55
Crisp, V. W., 53, 62, 63
Cross, S., 46
Cummings, E. M., 26, 27, 29, 30, 31, 32, 34, 35, 36, 37, 64n, 80
Cummings, J. S., 32

Daly, E. M., 63
Damhuis, I., 71
Davidson, R. J., 13
Davies, P., 19, 20, 26, 27, 30, 31, 34, 35, 36, 37
De Rivera, J., 6, 10, 70, 71
Demos, E. V., 6, 12
Denham, S. A., 63, 77
Denxin, N. K., 61
Derryberry, D., 45
Dickson, K. L., 5, 8, 14, 16
Dienstbier, R. A., 45

SUBJECT INDEX

Achievement/mastery, 74–75
Adult children of alcoholics (ACOAs), 33, 37
Affect regulation, 35–36
Affective organization theory, of parental socialization (Dix), 51–52
Alcoholism. *See* Children of alcoholics (COAs); Parental alcoholism
Asian infants. *See* Chinese infants; Japanese infants
Attachment model, of personality development (Bowlby), 50–51
Attachment relationship, 50–51
Attractors, 8–10. *See also* Communication frames

Behavior, emotion and, 45
Behavior problems: interadult conflict and, 31; internalizing of, 28
Brain: attractors and, 8–9; emotional development and, 9; ontogenetic changes in, 8

Change. *See* Developmental change
Child abuse, 33
Children of alcoholics (COAs): childhood problems of, 25; emotional regulation/coping, 27–28; interadult conflict and, 31–32, 36–39; internalizing behavior problems by, 28; psychopathology of, 25–26; statistics on, 25. *See also* Parental alcoholism
Chinese infants, studies of, 91–92. *See also* Infant emotions, observer judgment and (study)
Co-orientation, 11
Cognition, emotions and, 7, 45
Communication: co-orientation and, 11; linguistic, 12; social versus nonsocial, 11. *See also* Communication frames; Emotion communication
Communication frames: characteristics of, 11; defined, 11; emotional experience and, 20–21; examples of, 11; narrative and, 12; stability of, 11–12, 21
Constituents, emotional, 7–8
Creativity, emotional experience and, 10
Culture, family emotional expressiveness

and, 60–61; infant emotion and, 90–92; social emotions and, 70

Development: as change, 10–11; traditional view of, 10–11. *See also* Emotional development
Developmental change: dynamic systems approach to, 10, 21; emotional experience and, 10–11
Differential emotional theory, 6
Down's Syndrome, 60
Duchenne smile, 13–14, 17, 79
Duplay smile, 15–16, 17
Dynamic systems approach, emotional experience: emotions as change processes, 10–11; emotions as relational, 6–7; emotions as self-organizing systems, 7–10; reviews of, 5
Dynamic systems thinking, 10

Embarrassment, 69, 72–73
Emotion communication: achievement/mastery and, 74–75; boundary-setting and, 74, 80; changing views of, 1; child-parent relationship and, 73, 76–77; children's achievement/mastery and, 74–80; children's communication of needs/goals and, 73–74, 78–80; context and, 72–73; defined, 71; development of shame/pride/guilt and, 73–85; facial movements and, 72; feeling and, 73; functionalist theory and, 69; as interactive process, 71; intentionality of, 72; parental approval/disapproval and, 73–76; parental perception of children's responses and, 74, 84; positive, 77; pride versus mastery responses and, 82; regulatory function of, 71–72; rules/standards and, 74, 76–77; social emotional display and, 81–82; social motives and, 72; social referencing and, 75; as testing, 80; violation/adherence to social standards and, 74, 81–84
Emotion families, 69–70
Emotion measurement, 90
Emotion(s): attention/learning and, 45; behavior regulation and, 34–35; as change process, 10–11; children's

113

ORDERING INFORMATION

NEW DIRECTIONS FOR CHILD DEVELOPMENT is a series of paperback books that presents the latest research findings on all aspects of children's psychological development, including their cognitive, social, moral, and emotional growth. Books in the series are published quarterly in Fall, Winter, Spring, and Summer and are available for purchase by subscription and individually.

SUBSCRIPTIONS cost $65.00 for individuals (a savings of 23 percent over single-copy prices) and $105.00 for institutions, agencies, and libraries. Standing orders are accepted. New York residents, add local sales tax for subscriptions. (For subscriptions outside the United States, add $7.00 for shipping via surface mail or $25.00 for air mail. Orders *must be prepaid* in U.S. dollars by check drawn on a U.S. bank or charged to VISA, MasterCard, or American Express.)

SINGLE COPIES cost $25.00 plus shipping (see below) when payment accompanies order. California, New Jersey, New York, and Washington, D.C., residents, please include appropriate sales tax. Canadian residents, add GST and any local taxes. Billed orders will be charged shipping and handling. No billed shipments to post office boxes. (Orders from outside the United States *must be prepaid* in U.S. dollars by check drawn on a U.S. bank or charged to VISA, MasterCard, or American Express.)

SHIPPING (SINGLE COPIES ONLY): $30.00 and under, add $5.50; to $50.00, add $6.50; to $75.00, add $7.50; to $100.00, add $9.00; to $150.00, add $10.00.

ALL PRICES are subject to change.

DISCOUNTS FOR QUANTITY ORDERS are available. Please write to the address below for information.

ALL ORDERS must include either the name of an individual or an official purchase order number. Please submit your order as follows:
    Subscriptions: specify series and year subscription is to begin
    Single copies: include individual title code (such as CD59)

FOR SUBSCRIPTION SALES OUTSIDE OF THE UNITED STATES, contact any international subscription agency or Jossey-Bass directly.

MAIL ORDERS TO:
    Jossey-Bass Publishers
    350 Sansome Street
    San Francisco, California 94104-1342

PHONE subscription or single-copy orders toll-free at (888) 378-2537 or at (415) 433-1767 (toll call).

FAX orders toll-free to (800) 605-2665.